Fifty Years of Polyamory in America

Fifty Years of Polyamory in America

A Guided Tour of a Growing Movement

Glen W. Olson
and
Terry Lee Brussel-Rogers

ROWMAN & LITTLEFIELD
Lanham • Boulder • New York • London

Published by Rowman & Littlefield
An imprint of The Rowman & Littlefield Publishing Group, Inc.
4501 Forbes Boulevard, Suite 200, Lanham, Maryland 20706
www.rowman.com

86-90 Paul Street, London EC2A 4NE

British Library Cataloguing in Publication Information Available

Library of Congress Cataloging-in-Publication Data Available

ISBN 9781538169759 (cloth) | ISBN 9781538169766 (ebook)

Contents

Foreword

It was our senior wife, Morning Glory, who officially coined the terms *poly-amory* and *polyamorous*, in an article she wrote for the May 1990 issue of our Pagan magazine, *Green Egg*. This was followed by an extensive "Glossary of Relationship Terminology." The article was titled "A Bouquet of Lovers," written in response to a request from Diane, our third partner/wife of the time. Morning Glory was always referring to "the rules" of multiple relationships, and Diane, who was at the time "domineditrix" of the magazine, asked her to set them down in writing so everyone would know what they were.

In composing the article, Morning Glory needed a simple term to express the idea of having multiple simultaneous sexual/loving relationships without necessarily *marrying* everyone. This sounds so obvious, but strangely, there had never been any such word. Since *monogamy* means, literally, "marriage to one," the obvious corollary to that was *polygamy*, meaning "marriage to many." But she needed a word that simply meant "having multiple lovers."

Morning Glory and I had both studied Latin in high school and knew a smattering of Greek as well. When we needed to coin words, we naturally looked to Greek and Latin roots. However, the Latin for "loving many" would be *multi-amory*, which sounded awkward, and the Greek would be *polyphilia*, which sounded like a disease.

In discussing this semantic dilemma, Morning Glory had the brilliant insight to combine both Greek and Latin roots into *poly-amory*. This sounded just perfect. So she used it in the article. And the rest, as they say, is history.

Here is Morning Glory's definition, which she gave to the editor of the *Oxford English Dictionary* when they contacted her to enter the term:

> Polyamory: The practice, state or ability of having more than one sexual loving relationship at the same time, with the full knowledge and consent of all partners involved.

I believe that polyamory is a very important new relationship option whose time seems to have arrived. Where once we thought every family should consist of a monogamous man and woman with their 2.5 kids, we now consider a family to be any small group of bonded people who claim that connection with one another.

Many families today no longer fit that conventional description. The much-lamented "breakdown of the American family" and the call to reclaim "traditional family values" are manifestations of the twentieth-century transition from village life and extended families to the modern "nuclear family" units, which are often reduced to a single mother trying to raise and support children she hardly has time to interact with.

A century ago, the typical American family consisted of three generations (grandparents, parents, and children) living together in a large house, often along with lateral relatives such as uncles and aunts, and even at least one unrelated live-in nanny, butler, cook, or housekeeper. The "traditional American family," in fact, looked pretty much like *The Addams Family*!

Each generation in the last century became increasingly isolated and alienated. Ever-increasing numbers of American children are growing up with no brothers or sisters, hardly any parental interactions, and no adult role models for parenting or other relationships. Their interactions with other children occur in hostile environments, such as schools and the street, where they are subject to ever-rising levels of teasing, harassment, bullying, and violence. They retreat to the world of television, video games, and the internet—none of which provide real-life interaction with actual flesh-and-blood human beings.

But deep within each of us is our genetic ancestral memory of the tribe, the clan, the extended family. Such rich relationships nurtured and sustained our ancestors from the dawn of time, and it was within that context that we became fully human. We require and crave such connections and relationships in our deepest heart of hearts, and we seek them out in clubs, gangs, fraternities, cliques, parties, pubs, communes, churches, nests, covens, and circles of close friends.

An increasing number of us are learning how to create such complex and deep bonding relationships through extended networks of multiple lovers and expanded families. Polyamory, implying multiple lovers, is both a new paradigm for relationships and a vision for healing the pathological alienation of individuals in modern society.

Fifty Years of Polyamory in America by Glen W. Olson with Terry Lee Brussel-Rogers, presents an excellent perspective on the history of a significant new paradigm for relationships appropriate to the changes in culture we've seen over the last half century. I have personally been involved in many of these events during this period, and it's a pleasure to read this account and be able to attest to its accuracy. Step aboard, good reader, for a grand adventure!

May you never thirst!

Oberon Zell-Ravenheart
March 7, 2021

Acknowledgments

The authors would like to thank the many people who generously gave us their time for interviews and access to their documents while we were compiling this history of the polyamory movement.

Special thanks are given to:

Oberon Zell-Ravenheart, for writing the forward, the many hours of interviews he gave while we were writing our chapter on the Church of All Worlds, and his guidance on how to find a publisher. Thanks for the inspiration he has given to Terry Brussel-Rogers through his work in the Pagan community and the founding the Church of All Worlds, making real what Heinlein wrote in *Stranger in a Strange Land*. When Oberon speaks, it is an inspiration to all who hear him.

Morning Glory Zell-Ravenheart, for the article "A Bouquet of Lovers," the term *polyamory*, and her excellent example of living a poly lifestyle.

Pat Lafollette, for his historical knowledge of Family Synergy, both as cofounder and archivist, and for his valuable presentations to Live the Dream over the years.

Craig Milo Brussel-Rogers, for his assistance in editing this book for grammar and flow, for being Terry Brussel-Rogers's sounding board for much of its content, and for driving while she wrote.

Leanna Wolfe, for reading and reviewing our book with the eye of an anthropologist who has studied this subject for much of her professional life, and for providing fascinating presentations on polyamory throughout the world at Poly Conventions, Live the Dream meetings, and all manner of professional associations.

Paul Gibbons, for sharing materials from his videography of poly events over the last forty years and demonstrating, for all who are privileged to know him, a life without jealousy.

Robert A. Heinlein, for his books *Stranger in a Strange Land* through *To Sail Beyond the Sunset*, providing inspiration to many in the poly community, including the authors.

William H. Patterson Jr., for writing the fully researched biography of Robert A. Heinlein, which showed he lived the lifestyles he wrote about.

Deborah Anapol, who greatly benefited the poly community with her excellent writing on ethical nonmonogamy and her part in the formation of Loving More along with Ryam Nearing and its current organizer, Robyn Trask. Anapol's presentations for Live the Dream were always excellent, and we all learned from them. We are delighted to have our book accepted by the same publisher who published her book, *Polyamory in the 21st Century*.

Robert Rimmer, for his excellent contributions to polyamorous-oriented thinking through the novels *The Harrad Experiment*, *Proposition 31*, and many others, as well as his informative presentations to Live the Dream by phone. He was always available to Terry whenever she needed advice on how share this lifestyle with others.

Janet Hardy (AKA Lady Green), for her many contributions to the polyamory and alternate sexuality communities, both as the author of *The Ethical Slut* and as the founder/publisher of Greenery Press. She has given a voice to many authors who would otherwise have never been heard.

Jay Wiseman, for his many books and articles on open relationships and alternate sexuality, and for his advice on writing and how to read book contracts.

Larry and Joan Constantine, whose book *Group Marriage* provided well-researched information on this topic at a time when that was rare. Terry's personal experience with Larry and Joan at a Family Synergy conference in the 1980s greatly enhanced her knowledge of working group marriages that stayed together!

Stan Dale, for his creation of the Sex, Love, and Intimacy HAI workshops, which led to many personal revelations on communication and how it applies to poly relationships. Thanks also to his wife Helen Dale—whose heartwarming examples of compersion included announcing at an HAI function that she wanted her co-wife Janet to become Stan's legal wife while she became the co-wife—for encouraging   Terry's personal connection with Stan for many years. Helen was a caring and knowledgeable listener, sympathetic to Terry's own challenges with organizing poly education and outreach programs.

Susan Olson, for her unwavering support during this project, and her expert help with the technical aspects of the computer programs and apps required to write a book in the modern era.

1

What Is Polyamory and What Is It Doing to America?

Most of us are familiar with the term *monogamy*. Often connected with marriage or another committed relationship, it is a contract between two people who agree that they will have sex only with each other. It is the most prevalent form of emotional/sexual relationship between two people in Western cultures and is believed to be sanctioned by all modern Judeo-Christian religions.

But monogamy is not the only emotional/sexual relationship style people can choose. *Polyamory* is a term coined in 1990 by Morning Glory Zell in an article she wrote to address the ethical problems that can often occur in multiply committed relationships,[1] that is to say, a situation where one person has two or more acknowledged sexual relationships at the same time.

Dr. Deborah Anapol embraced the term and used it to teach about relationships that could include—but did not necessarily include—marriage.[2] In its broadest sense, the word *polyamory* may be used to describe every form of multiple lover/spouse arrangement people enter into. Everything that is not an agreed-upon monogamous relationship can be described by the Greek prefix *poly*—meaning "many"—and *amor*, Latin for sexual love.

Throughout the pages of this book, we will meet many people who use the term *polyamory*—and we will find they do not always mean the same thing by it. Some people have much narrower definitions of what it is "they" do as poly people, distinct from what "other people" do. In the end, we may respectfully come to some consensus of what the word means; if not, we will at least have a better understanding of what people have been doing for the last fifty years.

1

When did Americans begin practicing polyamory? Is this style of loving brand-new or has it in fact been around for a long time? A better question to start with might be: Was there ever a time on this continent when people did *not* practice some form of multiple-partner arrangement?

A quick perusal through the history books shows us that some Americans have in fact experimented with all kinds of multiple-partner life and love situations—and have even in some cases called them "marriage." One well-known experiment in cooperative living, economic entrepreneurship, and shared spouses began in a sleepy part of rural New York in 1848. The Oneida Community began as one man's vision of the perfect form of Christian living and eventually became a powerhouse of economic success and stability for several hundred people, all of whom practiced a form of relationship called *complex marriage.*[3]

John Humphrey Noyes was born in Brattleboro, Vermont, in 1811. Originally headed for a career in law, he was swept up in the religious revival of the period and instead became a minister. After years of perfecting his philosophies on social utopias and religious freedom, he gathered a following and founded what was essentially a commune outside of Oneida, New York. He based the precepts of the group upon what he believed God wanted from a good Christian.

The members of the Oneida Community adopted Noyes's philosophies and implemented his vision of complex marriage in 1848. A complex marriage is one where every woman in the community is wife to every man, and every man is husband to every woman. The Oneidas also believed strongly in a form of free love, where any adult was free to have sex with any other consenting adult in the community. Possessiveness and exclusive relationships were frowned upon and actively discouraged by the community leadership.

While sex was not limited to one partner, it was also not just for pleasure. The Oneidas believed strongly that raising children was a sacred shared responsibility and that the decision to have a child was not solely up to the individual. Instead, the community chose with whom, and when, the individual conceived a child.[4]

The Oneida Community lasted more than thirty years, growing to include more than two hundred adults and a myriad of children. It provided homes and livelihood for its members by owning and successfully operating farms, a trapping company, and a silver-working company. (Yes, *that* Oneida; for many years Oneida was synonymous with silverware.)

Even after the Oneida Community broke up and the participants reorganized into more traditional marriages, the legacy lived on. As its final action, the community provided funds for all the children who had not reached adulthood to get a start in life, providing advanced educations for them as well.

Science fiction author Robert A. Heinlein (1907–1988) is one of several authors often referenced by large segments of the polyamory community for his many novels with multiple spouse/lover themes. He has stated in his books his opinion that marriage has two functions: the conservation of wealth and protection of children. He may have been thinking in part of the Oneida Community when he made these observations.

Even before Oneida, in the 1820s, another powerful experiment in nonmonogamy began in upstate New York when Joseph Smith founded a religious movement that would come to be called the Church of Jesus Christ of Latter-day Saints, sometimes called Mormonism. One of the many tenets of the revealed word of God in this movement instructed the elders to take more than one wife. To be very clear, the reverse was not true: women were not instructed to have several husbands. The Mormons faced many trials, eventually moving to Utah Territory, where they thrived and nearly succeeded creating a state where their form of nonmonogamy, called *plural marriage*, would be legal.

The present-day Church of Jesus Christ of Latter-day Saints no longer actively permits its members to engage in plural marriage, a form of religious polygamy. However, as recently as 2019 the media reported that a Mormon enclave in Mexico still openly practices plural marriage—and many Mormons may in fact still practice this aspect of their religion informally.[5] (It is also a great American tradition to ignore what your church elders tell you to do and go ahead and do whatever you want to anyway!)

Colonial America was a time of great exploration and expansion as settlers from the great European nations came to the shores of North America to found colonies, originally along the east coast of the continent. Of course, this land was already inhabited! The powerful Iroquois Confederacy found throughout what is now upstate New York and the Powhatans of the Hudson Bay region had strikingly different marriage customs than the Europeans, who found it very disturbing that Powhatan men were allowed to have many wives.[6]

Notice that we have said that these examples meet the definition of nonmonogamy. They may in fact not meet our modern definition of *polyamory*. But more on that later; in the meantime, let us jump a few hundred years or so ahead to the present time.

In 1967 an event took place that was destined to shake American society to its foundations and cause not just isolated splinter groups, but huge segments of the population to pay attention, to wonder, and to ultimately question their relationships with themselves and with the people they loved.

The Summer of Love was the culmination of three dominant trends happening in America at the time. The civil rights movement had been changing people's hearts throughout the 1960s, making activism respectable. The

Human Potential Movement, coming from good old American philosophical and psychological roots, had been quietly gaining momentum all decade long with the message that you can change who you are for the better. And the literary Beat culture of the 1950s, whose basic tenets included challenging your preconceptions, making a spiritual quest, and rejecting economic materialism had turned into the popular and energetic hippie movement of the 1960s.

The result was an event and a movement—literally. In the spring and summer of 1967, thousands of young people migrated to New York City and San Francisco, California, to attend weeks-long "happenings" that celebrated music, drugs, personal expression, and free love.

Some of these young people had a deep distrust of government as they perceived it, along with a strong desire to change society—and they started by changing themselves and how they related to one another. They also poured a lot of energy into the antiwar movement of the late 1960s and early 1970s. One slogan from that era that continues to resonate through the years is "Make Love, Not War."

The fervor of these secular movements infused the following decades with excitement about human potential and the ability of humans to love. Many people who were otherwise happy and content with the society they were living in began personal explorations that led them to include new ideas about what love and caring might look like and making broader choices in their personal lives.

Something unique in human history happened at this point. A few people began questioning the idea that marriage was to be limited to only two people. Not only could someone have more than one lover, perhaps they could have more than one spouse. In chapter 4 we will introduce you to Family Synergy, a group formed in 1971 that explored this concept deeply and learned a lot.

What was unique about the concept of polyamory at this time in history? We have already shown that marriages of more than two people have existed through the ages. But polyamory is not based on the religious precepts of an Oneida or Mormon movement, nor on any prior Christian or non-Christian philosophy. Polyamory is not even driven by a deep cultural/economic necessity, like many styles of marriage the world has seen.

What do we mean by cultural necessity? Anthropologist Leanna Wolfe, author of *Women Who May Never Marry*,[7] has made a study of women's roles around the world, particularly what it means to be a married woman in dozens of very different societies. She also gives seminars on the various types of marriage found in these cultures and hazards guesses as to why they may have developed that way. For instance, in traditional Tibetan society, two brothers may choose to marry the same woman, making three. Well, that doesn't sound like monogamy, does it? But why would two brothers choose to marry one woman?

There turns out to be a very sound economic reason for this arrangement: if two brothers share a wife, the accumulated family wealth remains intact. Instead of two families each taking a smaller portion of the farm or family business, there is only one family and it does not get poorer. This is a good thing in a culture where there is very little wealth and no economic safety nets.

Does the woman in question really want two husbands? Perhaps, but would she pick those two particular men if there were not serious economic pressures pushing her that way? And would they choose her in return or make a different choice? In America, by contrast, whom you sleep with and whom you marry has become a very personal choice!

Our interviews with many people in the polyamory movement over the years, and our analysis of the movement, have led us to conclude that for the right person, polyamory can be a positive lifestyle choice. This is the history we will primarily show in these pages. Like every lifestyle choice, polyamory is not a good fit for everyone. Throughout this book we will cover the challenges and drawbacks of this lifestyle.

This is the journey we hope to chronicle here for the enjoyment and education of the reader. Perhaps you will find yourself somewhere in these pages—or wind up using them as a guidepost for the next exciting phase of your own life.

2

Becoming Poly

Perhaps a further definition of *polyamory* would be helpful here. In the early days of the movement, when people were grappling for a way to describe what they were trying to do, many phrases were used, such as *open relationship* and *open marriage*. One of the most descriptive was *responsible nonmonogamy*. Dr. Deborah Anapol takes three pages in her book *Polyamory: The New Love without Limits* to define terms such as *ethical nonmonogamy, open relationship,* and *open marriage* and apply these concepts to the new term *polyamory*.[1] Over and over again she points out that people are using specific principles to guide their behavior with other people.

We analyzed her explanation and believe we can boil it down to this statement: To be polyamorous is to consciously choose to have—or be open to having—emotional bonds with more than one lover at the same time and to ethically manage those relationships.

The ethical management part is key. There are many types of multiple-partner sexual behavior—and we are not criticizing anyone for their choices here, but if you are being secretive with your lovers, lying to them about what you are doing, or managing information so one doesn't know about the other(s), then what you are doing doesn't meet the criteria for polyamory.

So how does a person become polyamorous? Do they wake up one morning with the realization, "Hey, I'm poly"? Might the person have a vague awareness in the back of their mind, from a very young age, that loving more than one person at a time makes sense to them? Or is it a journey of small steps, an awareness that something more is wanted or needed in their lives? Does the epiphany come from reading a book, having a casual conversation with a friend, seeing a TV show, finding a site online, or perhaps hearing a news item about a "swingers ranch" or "nudist resort"?

The answer is yes—all of the above. Somehow the awareness that more is possible comes to the person, and the route to realization of this aspect of their lives is as individual as the people themselves.

Dee is thirty-four years old and has met with me (Glen) at the local coffee emporium for tea and conversation. She is a nurse, a very attractive Hindu woman who grew up in India and London. Her accent is a delicious blend of her two nationalities. Her parents are deeply traditional and talked her into accepting an arranged marriage at age twenty-four to a man she met only once. She has been married ten years and has one child. She wants to talk about her marriage.

> I think there is something missing in my marriage; I *know* there is something missing in my marriage. I learned to love my husband, and I do love him. To me, love is a thing we choose to do as much as it is an emotion.
> But lately I want more excitement in my marriage, and I want another child. My husband doesn't want me to have another baby; he likes that we just have one.

"I don't understand my American girlfriends," she goes on to say. It turns out that all of her American girlfriends are giving her the same advice: dump the husband, walk away from the marriage, and marry someone else who will give her more children. She knows there is something wrong with this advice, and she is very frustrated.

"I don't want to give up the things I've got. I have a good husband; I am happy in so many ways . . . I just wish he would have an affair or something. I want him to be more adventurous and make our lives more exciting."

On my side of the table, I'm blinking in shock. She wants her husband to have an *affair* to get their marriage out of the rut it is in? Wow! During these conversations, I'm rarely impelled to give advice, although I might offer information and talk about the choices other people make, but in this case I make an exception. I tell her she needs to dump her American girlfriends, not her husband. Her friends do not have her best interests at heart, and I think her instincts to work within her marriage, to strengthen and grow *with* her husband, is the right choice.

Amazingly, she takes my advice. About six months later we are having another conversation and she confides that she is deliriously back in love with her husband and life is extremely exciting for them—but wait, here is the rest of the story: Her husband was not interested in going out to find a woman to have an *affair* with, but after some deep and intimate conversations she admitted to him that she had always felt she might be bisexual and was interested in exploring that. He gave his blessing to her seeing if she wanted a female lover, and now she has a soft, cuddly woman in her life and still has the man she wanted to keep all along.

Another route to polyamory is Terry's story. She had a defining episode as a teenager that helped her realize that she was, simply, naturally polyamorous. She explains:

> I wonder at times if part of my interest in polyamory came from an experience I had at sixteen, which really gave me insight into myself. I had already read the book *Stranger in a Strange Land*, where Robert Heinlein writes about multiple relationships, but no one I knew was doing it. I broke up with my boyfriend because I was interested in someone else. Even though I was the one ending the relationship, I could not deal with it emotionally; it was too painful—he had to hold me while I cried hysterically, when I should have been comforting him! Even though I thought I was following the cultural norm and had to do it that way, it didn't make me happy.
>
> I have rarely had to go through that as the one doing the breaking up for that reason as an adult. While I have had to handle men breaking up with me, which has hurt deeply, I have never had to deal with doing such a thing to *myself* as well as to my partner by breaking off one relationship to start a new one. This does not have to happen when all involved are committed to the concept of being able to love and be committed to more than one significant other. It is even possible to join together in a group house, thereby not having to choose only one beloved with whom to live. I have been in nonmonogamous relationships throughout my adult life. I believe in inclusive rather than exclusive relationships. For me, this certainly makes more sense and causes far less pain than that portrayed in so much of our literature as love triangles, which feature jealous fighting between two men wanting one woman or two women clawing at each other over the male object of their affections.

In Dee's case, all her seeking and explorations occurred in a very personal way and one-by-one contacts. She didn't join any organizations, read any books, or turn her life upside down to get what she wanted. She knew something was missing and was questing for the answer. She met one person with some knowledge to share. This is the route for a huge number of people. But others like Terry, having trouble finding what they want, wind up finding networks and organizations to join, or in some cases start those organizations themselves.

A number of networks, associations, and clubs dealing with people's increased interest in improving their sex lives began in the early years of the 1970s. We will introduce you to some of these very influential organizations from this time period. They often began with very different goals and were attractive to different people, but with a lot of overlap.

Morehouse or More University, also called the Institute of Human Abilities, was founded in 1968 by Dr. Victor Baranco and his wife, Dr. Suzanne Baranco. The Human Awareness Institute (HAI), started by Stan and Helen Dale, and the Church of All Worlds, started by Oberon Zell, also had their beginning in 1968.

Family Synergy was founded in May of 1971 by a small group of people who were originally interested in discussing how to form group marriages. Synergy grew into a large, diverse educational organization that connected other organizations and served the needs of many groups of people exploring alternative relationships.

Down through the years, other organizations were born and came to prominence. In 1987, Live the Dream was created by Terry Lee Brussel-Rogers. In 1992 Dr Deborah Anapol began teaching her Love Without Limits workshops; she subsequently launched Loving More with Ryam Nearing in 1994.

Then, in 2012, a book hit the bookstores that fired a shot heard round the world. The book was *Sex at Dawn: How We Mate, Why We Stray, and What It Means for Modern Relationships*. In this book, Chris Ryan and Cacilda Jetha posit that current Western customs of monogamy are just that—customs, having nothing to do with genetic wiring, male versus female mating patterns, or instinct.

Using modern methods of biology, sociology, and anthropology, Ryan and Jetha make a pretty good case that what we are taught to believe we want and what human beings actually desire are very different. One question they tackle is, Are human beings *naturally* monogamous? Better yet, they tackle the question whether any animal species can be shown to be wired for monogamy.[2]

Modern biologists have a few advantages over Charles Darwin, who had to rely on his powers of observation and admittedly brilliant mind. DNA testing is very helpful in determining parentage, whether you are a human or a swan. And what have modern biologists determined?

Our little friend the prairie vole, who bonds deeply with, and refuses to sit with, any vole who is not its mate, will in fact sleep around. A significant percentage of their offspring are genetically someone else's. That other paragon of virtue, the penguin, who with her mate will stave off the fierce Antarctic blasts to protect nest and egg, nurture the little one together, and as a family, shepherd it safely to the sea when it is old enough to forage for itself, has a one-season relationship. Next year the two will likely pick other mates and do it all over again.

And need we bring up the majestic swan, that creature of beauty and grace that typifies the title of lovebird? If you are a poet, you might be sad to learn that swans are not in the tiny percentage of bird species that are apparently monogamous.

So, to bring this chapter to a close, we try to answer the question that began it: How do people become polyamorous? Apparently, the same way they become monogamous: by choosing to.

3

Why Do You People Do This—
Are You All Nuts?

Funny you should ask. Americans are widely regarded around the world as crazy—in many ways. We have this excessive desire to be our own person, not follow the crowd, not slavishly follow tradition—just because our parent was a miner in the coal mines of Pennsylvania doesn't mean we must be too. We might become a doctor, lawyer, senator, or CEO. We might follow in our family footsteps—but then again, we might not.

We also have this extreme desire to champion the truth, see justice served, promote freedom in every heart, and place law over might. One event crystalized this understanding of who we Americans are and how many other nations of the world look at us. This seminal event took place at the turn of the millennium:

The 2000 general election and apparent irregularities in the Florida vote count cast a pall over the legitimacy of the US election process. A lot of people thought one of the political parties was cheating and attempting to steal the presidential election. For days the world watched as the Florida courts sought to certify the vote. When the decision came down, the Republicans were awarded Florida's electoral votes—and won the presidency of the United States.

CNN and other news networks showed worldwide reaction—mainly disbelief. From Russia to the Middle East to Europe to South America, people expected tanks to roll across America and civil war to break out. Many could not understand why it didn't happen. It didn't happen because this is America—and Americans believe in some crazy things, like fair play and upholding our system of laws.

Now we get to sex. This is where many of our European (and Asian and South American) counterparts start shaking their heads and murmuring, "What is it about Americans and sex?" And that's a darn good question.

Is it crazy to be the kind of person who discovers they can be sexually attracted to a new love and still be in love with their spouse or significant other? Not a bit, we see it all the time. Is it even strange to discover that we might actually have sex with a new lover and then go home and find we are still in love with our spouse or significant other? Nope, no problem; people obviously have the capacity to do that.

But how often is it okay for our spouse or significant other to welcome us home, knowing we have spent intimate time with another person, be happy for us—and still be in love with us? Perhaps more often than the press, movies, trashy romance novels, or other media would have us believe.

People who discover they are polyamorous find they can take joy in their loved one's having a wonderful experience with another lover and that when their loved one comes home the relationship is not damaged. Indeed, it is possible that the relationship is strengthened. A word was even coined for this feeling: it is called *compersion*.[1]

But be careful: in America it might be crazy to like sex. Since the 1950s, psychiatrists have become ever more interested in defining certain sexual practices as treatable illness. The American Psychiatric Association (APA) publishes the *Diagnostic and Statistical Manual* (DSM) to aid clinicians in diagnosing and treating psychiatric disorders. The DSM-II, released in 1968, listed 168 disorders and identified nymphomania and homosexuality as mental illnesses.

To give you an idea about how doctors define mental illness, as soon as the DSM-II was published in 1968, a strong minority of mental health professionals joined forces with activists from the gay rights movement and went to bat to get the diagnosis changed. In 1970, the APA reversed itself on the topic of homosexuality, and the DSM-III made no mention of sexual orientation as a treatable illness.[2]

However, nymphomania and its male corollary, satyriasis, had no such champions, and doctors remain very interested in treating them to this day. *Webster's Encyclopedic Unabridged Dictionary of the English Language* defines *nymphomania* as "abnormal and uncontrollable sexual desire in women."[3] Presumably, the "abnormal" part is wanting to have sex with more than one partner. And "uncontrollable"? In what manner? By whom?

As of this writing the DSM-5 is out, and this most recent update to the manual includes a grouping of sexual addictions called "hypersexuality disorder." Addictions of various types do exist, of course. Addictions like alcohol, drugs, overeating, and gambling require specific treatments and can ruin one's life without intervention. The inclusion of hypersexuality disorder in this well-used and respected publication might pose the danger of encouraging therapists and others to conclude that a person choosing multiple partners is exhibiting compulsive behavior.

In Terry's experience in her private hypnotherapy practice, most people who are afraid they have a sexual addiction are really quite normal. They may be struggling with a self-image issue or childhood religious dictates of behavior that are just not in line with average human behavior. Sometimes accusations of sex addiction come from people who are offended that someone is getting more sex than they are. Sometimes there is a spouse or significant other who simply has a lower sex drive than their partner. In those rare cases where an addiction really is present, the need for help is very real.

BUT ISN'T IT ILLEGAL?

That is a really good question. There have been times and places in this country where almost anything you can imagine has been declared illegal. If enough people didn't like something in a given community, they could proscribe it, with sometimes silly, sometimes tragic results.

If we take our time machine back only a bit more than a hundred years, to the year 1917, we will find a hodgepodge of laws in the forty-eight states about who may marry whom, at what ages, and under what circumstances. Only about eighteen of the forty-eight states allowed whites to marry nonwhites (the laws of the time presumed there were three racial groups: white, black, and brown) and if you were married to someone of another race and you entered a state that did not allow mixed marriages, there was no reciprocity. In the eyes of that state, you were not married, and worse, you could be arrested and charged with a crime for having committed mixed marriage elsewhere.

Between 1917 and 1967, another thirteen states changed their laws to allow mixed marriages, but it was not until the 1967 Supreme Court decision *Loving v. Virginia* that any adult of any race could marry an adult of the opposite sex who was of a different race. Perhaps not coincidentally, 1967 is the very year our particular history of polyamory begins. In terms of social movements, that is not very long ago. And there's another historical footnote that might interest you: In 1917 women did not yet have the right to vote. That occurred by amendment to the constitution in 1920.

The year 1967 was a landmark in the quest to allow people the right to choose whom they love and marry, but there was much left to be done. The civil rights movement had won a great victory when *Loving* struck down the remaining miscegenation laws, but it was still a crime in nearly every corner of the country to engage in sex with someone of your own gender. It took gay rights activists another fifty years to achieve the same legal status that heterosexuals now took for granted.

The good news first: as of the publication of this book, sex between single, consenting adults, whether of the same sex or not, is legal in all fifty states and the several territories of the United States. More good news—or at least we, the authors, think this is good news: as of 2015, almost fifty years after the landmark Supreme Court decision in *Loving*, two adults of the same gender may now legally enter into marriage together anywhere within the United States.

It was a long time between that first landmark step, striking down the vestiges of the antimiscegenation laws, and the second step concerning allowable sexual conduct and who may marry whom. It has been a long, hard battle for change, and the people who found themselves on the front lines risked much. These battles came with a great deal of risk: damage to one's reputation, loss of job or other financial harm, loss of one's children to child protective services, and even imprisonment. Society's attitudes are still in flux, but some legal protections now do exist.

And yes, some things are still illegal.

Bigamy, on its face, is a crime of fraud: fraud against the unwitting partner and fraud against the state. (This presumes the bigamist is not being transparent; there is no fraud involved against the partner if everyone is informed and consenting, yet it is still a crime according to the state.) It is still the law of the land that you can be legally married to only one person at a time. If you file marriage papers with a state and you already have a legal marriage in effect anywhere else in the United States, that is a crime.

Some people commit bigamy as an act of carelessness, perhaps abandoning a marriage somewhat informally and simply failing to go through the divorce process to dissolve the marriage, then failing to disclose that to the next person they marry. Other people deliberately engage in a deception and marry a second spouse in order to gain access to a person's wealth or resources that they would not get otherwise. Sometimes an individual who regularly travels out of town for work actually leads a double life, with a spouse and perhaps children in each city or country where they regularly spend time.

In all these cases, the spouse has no idea they are not the only one, and they are very often shocked and very upset when they find out. They did not consent to be part of a multiple arrangement and may even find themselves economically harmed. They have truly been defrauded.

Many specific rights and privileges come with marriage, including inheritance rights, accrual of shared property, access to medical care, and the ability to make medical decisions for a spouse who becomes incapacitated and unable to make their own decisions.

The whole body of civil law concerning marriage contracts presumes that it is a contract between two people only. These legal protections have no exceptions. The state literally has no framework to consider anything else. This makes it impossible for individuals who might want to choose marriage honorably and openly with more than one spouse to actually be able to build such relationships.

This is an issue that will appear in other places in this book, as it has tripped up some very sincere poly people who have no desire to defraud anyone, who practice open loving communication with their lovers, and who are just trying to increase the joy in their lives.

Adultery—in the legal sense, not the biblical one—is still with us. Unlike bigamy, the concept of adultery as a crime was never as enduring, and over time has disappeared from most state legal codes. But it still exists in some forms, in some places, and has definite consequences for some people.

Perhaps a definition is in order; pulling out our handy Merriam-Webster, we learn that adultery is "voluntary sexual intercourse between a married man and someone other than his wife or between a married woman and someone other than her husband."[4] So the offending party has to be married for adultery to have occurred. Well, that narrows it down: this is cheating with the added dimension of matrimony.

Although adultery is a misdemeanor in most states that have laws against it, some, like Michigan and Wisconsin, categorize it as a felony. The criminal penalties for adultery range from the laughable to the terribly unjust. In the state of Maryland, you can receive a civil fine of about ten dollars; in Massachusetts, up to three years in jail and a much heftier fine. While adultery laws are on the books in a number of locales, it is commonly believed that they are never enforced these days and will probably never be enforced again.[5]

So why do they still have any relevance? They still matter in at least three social arenas. In states that have an adversarial divorce system, adultery is one of the reasons you can petition the court to dissolve your marriage. In these cases, the accused adulterer is at a serious disadvantage in front of the court, with penalties that include a reduction in the amount of common property granted and loss of child support, child custody, or alimony.

There are other situations where people in the United States who are leading nonstandard or nonmonogamous lifestyles risk confrontation with governmental agencies like child protective services and have sometimes lost their children, occasionally for extended periods of time, while having to prove they are fit parents. This happened with greater frequency in the 1970s and

1980s before society became more comfortable with the nonstandard modes of family (like same-sex parents and poly parents) that have been developing for the last fifty years. But it can and does still happen. It is something to be aware of even today.

There is another issue to raise here. Every adult that is responsible for raising children winds up making choices that affect their children's lives. This is true of every lifestyle. Much has been written about how children are affected in single-parent families by their parent's choices in dating and partnering. More is starting to be learned about children in poly families.

Not all children have good experiences in multiple adult situations, and some may even be harmed by their parents' choices. This social movement has existed long enough that children who have grown up in poly families, with multiple adults in their lives, have started being studied by professionals and have begun documenting their experiences. Many children report positive experiences, but not all.

The military is another culture where perceived sexual misconduct such as adultery can result in loss of position or rank, sometimes even forcing the offender into early retirement. Clearly there are penalties for perceived unethical behavior.

So that is the sad part of our tale. Now we would like to talk about the people who are intent upon forging a new set of social norms and are championing ethical behaviors that will enrich and improve their lives.

WHY DO SOME PEOPLE "DO" POLYAMORY?

The reasons people engage in polyamory are as varied as the people themselves. Sociologist Elisabeth Sheff did a groundbreaking fifteen-year study on the practice of polyamory, with special emphasis on families with children. In some cases, she was able to follow the same families for many years. She is also CEO/director of the Sheff Consulting Group, a think tank in Atlanta that advises policy makers on issues involving unconventional and underserved populations.

In her book *The Polyamorists Next Door*,[6] Sheff identifies six major factors most of her study population cited as the reason they participate (or at one time participated) in a poly lifestyle: getting more needs met, more love in their lives, sexual variety, family expansion, rebellion, and, for some, it just feels natural.

Let's expand on those a little, shall we? At first blush, getting more needs met, more love, and more sex could sound like the same thing, but they're really not, and the distinctions are illuminating. (By the way, we the authors identify with most of these needs ourselves.) Time and again these topics come up in poly workshops that both authors have attended or led over the years. Terry has also written extensively in venues like *Loving More* magazine and the Family Synergy and Live the Dream newsletters, and has given national interviews on these topics.

Getting More Needs Met

Modern life in our ever-changing society is a complex and complicated dance of work, play, family life, and relationships. How many times in a traditionally structured relationship have you heard someone—usually the woman—say, "I need a wife"?

The tasks and duties (and choices) in our modern world take up so much time and energy that we are left feeling the need for a little bit more help than our spouse or significant other can give us. This feeling of scarcity is usually not examined further, because to do so the person might have to face the possibility that they truly have unmet needs—and that all those needs cannot be reasonably expected to be fulfilled by the other person in the relationship. Sometimes the need is for sex itself, but sometimes it is for other types of intimacy.

Many poly people cite this realization—that it is unfair of them to demand the other person in their relationship be all the things they need them to be—as the moment they decided they needed to open up their relationship horizons.

When Terry was a young mother in her early twenties, her needs were more easily met because she and her husband were in an open relationship. One of the agreements she had with her husband was that she could have other lovers and do social activities with them. She could ask for what she wanted—and what she wanted was to go dancing.

Since dancing was one activity her primary partner had no enthusiasm for, she went hunting for someone who would take her dancing. She found a man who was a former Arthur Murray instructor. He was a superb dancer and was also in the poly lifestyle.

Glen's unmet need at age twenty-eight was a little more complex. He needed a whole community. His wife had won a slot in a prestigious graduate school, an eight-hour drive away, while he had a geographically fixed job working for a fire department. She could go away Monday through Friday, returning home only for scant weekends, or he could move with her. He wanted her to be happy, but did not want to be a husband only on the weekends or give up his dream job. The question was, How do you have everything at the same time?

It helped that Glen's wife had friends and previous lovers in the city where the graduate school was located and they both had friends and lovers at home, and he had a job with an unusual amount of flexibility. The solution? They moved to the new city, she renewed her relationships, and he commuted.

Why did it work? Partly because Glen's dream job allowed for enormous flexibility. He could work several twenty-four-hour shifts in a row at the fire station, take a day off and do it again, performing a month's work in two weeks—and then go home. It really succeeded because friends and lovers supported them both in both locations. Glen could stay at a lover's home on his night off, and his wife had friends, companionship, and lovers helping her out when he was gone.

More Love

Many people have the capacity to be "in love," to experience that heady heart-deep complex of emotions that bonds one person to another. However, a lot of people have also experienced that somewhat unsettling (in this society) feeling that while they are already in love with someone, another person has entered their horizon and they start to feel surprisingly strong emotions about them, too. Egad! Could they be falling in love again? "But I'm already in love," they think. This is a common plot device in movies and books, the conundrum being, "What do I do? How do I choose?"

Some people eventually realize that for them, there really is no conflict; they have the capacity to be in love with two (or more) people at the same time, no matter what society says. And if the ability is there, some people want to embrace the reality. They do not always have to choose one person over another; sometimes they can keep both. They can have it all.

The corollary to this is that some people joyously find that it is okay for more than one person to be in love with them at the same time, too. Catastrophe does not have to ensue; we are able to make our own happy endings.

Sexual Variety

This is the aspect of polyamory that gets the most press and it is certainly important to many poly people to have the ability—and the right/permission—to have a variety of lovers. Sometimes this includes different loving styles. In our experience, every relationship between two people is unique, including the experience of sex with that person. There is a saying attributed to the Greek philosopher Heraclitus, "No man ever steps into the same river twice, for it is not the same river and he is not the same man."

Essentially, what we mean is that different lovers can help an individual have different experiences and get different needs met. As some people will want to go dancing, to the opera, or the ball game, each lover will have a style, sense of play, and range of desires that are uniquely their own, and here the differences can be wonderful.

Rhonda, a small business owner, was head over heels in love with Bob, her business partner and husband of fifteen years, and loved to do everything with him. But sex was very frustrating for her. They were both submissive sexually and were both pleasers. They tried very hard to please each other—when they weren't trying to get their needs met by pushing the other person to be sexually dominant.

When they opened up their marriage, it was a relief for both of them. Both Rhonda and Bob chose dominant lovers and made sure to arrange the calendar so they were out with their lovers on the same night. The next morning, they would both rush home to be with each other and bring all the sexy loving energy they had generated the night before with them. They were among the happiest couples Glen can remember meeting.

Family Expansion

The quest for more "family by choice" is a common theme when poly people get together to talk about their lives. In chapter 4 we will meet the folks from Family Synergy, a group founded on the belief that children and adults thrive better in larger, loving family groups. They believe that *you can* pick your family, or at least pick the people you are going to add to your family and share experiences with as if they are family. The definitions of *family* have also expanded with time; poly people use terms like *primary, secondary, tertiary, nesting* and *nonnesting relationships, pods, tribes,* and of course *family* when describing their lives.[7]

Rachel Hope, author of the book *Family by Choice: Platonic Partnered Parenting,*[8] offers the idea that one can choose a great parent to raise children with. The other biological parent is not your only choice.

Rebellion

People who choose polyamory (or other types of nonmonogamy) occasionally admit they started because they were rebelling against their parents' way of life. They sometimes describe choosing this form of love style as a reaction to very strict religious upbringing that has an antisexual message or bias. They may see it as the ultimate in rebellion to bring home two wives or a wife *and* husband to meet the parents.

Interestingly, polyamory has been around long enough for a couple of generations of children to have the opportunity to grow up in poly households—and yes, children of poly parents have also sometimes stated, quite vehemently, that they are *not* going to do what their parents are doing. They rebelliously say that monogamy is what's right for them.

It Feels Natural

When some people try to describe to nonpoly people why they are poly, words seem to fail them and they say things like, "I just feel poly; I have always felt that way." In the previous chapter we mentioned that the way to become poly is simple: just choose to be poly. If only it were that simple for some people.

One of our acquaintances is Jill, a vivacious and highly intelligent woman who has been in the poly community for many years. She was always puzzled as a teenager that none of her boyfriends ever seemed to want her to set up threesomes with her and a girlfriend. She loved both men and women; why couldn't they love each other like she did?

It bothered her so much that she went into the study of brain chemistry and how people fall in love. She has shared what she learned at numerous poly group talks and especially at workshops or seminars that talk about jealousy.

It seems that the brain's biochemistry and pheromones, and even the state of your immune system, have a lot to do with who you fall in love with and how you fall in love. She uses the term *attachment* to describe this partnering pattern. There is also a psychological concept called *attachment theory* that concentrates on childhood experiences and their influence on adult personality. In attachment theory, people who bonded well to their parents and caregivers in childhood are *secure attachment* types and people who had difficulties may turn out to be *anxious attachment* people. For your reading pleasure, attachment in polyamory is also explored in psychotherapist Jessica Fern's book *PolySecure* (2021).[9]

Jill's conclusion was that people whose biochemistry causes them to be high-attachment types tend to fall in love with a person and then find it literally painful to be separate from them. They think about the other person all the time and want to spend as much time as possible with them. This sounds like the ideal of romantic love so far, but let's take it a little further.

If you are a high-attachment person you will also tend to be very possessive. The mere thought that the other person might have feelings for anyone else is disturbing, and if that person is perceived as actually giving affection that you crave to someone else it is physically, viscerally painful. A person with high-attachment biochemistry will have a very hard time feeling good about their partner having other lovers, even if their partner is truly, deeply in love with them and places them first in every way.

Conversely, the low-attachment person is absolutely as capable of falling deeply in love but does not have the same experience of privation when away from their partner. For a low-attachment person, the concept that their partner may want to give affection or even make love to someone else does not cause visceral, physical discomfort.

Anybody can experience pangs of jealousy, possessiveness, or fear of loss; it doesn't matter if you are high or low attachment. But it is sometimes easier to see the facts of what is happening and far easier to make rational decisions if your body is not automatically pushing you into panic mode.

Can only low-attachment types make good poly people? Absolutely not. There are a lot of great reasons someone may choose to be polyamorous and embrace more in their lives. We will read their stories and hear about their paths throughout the rest of the book. In fact, in chapter 5 we will meet a whole bunch of people who take "more" to a whole new level.

The Accidental Polyamorist

There is one more category of polyamorist that is so ubiquitous the authors missed it as a separate category for years, even though we heard people say it in conversation over and over again. The person would say something like, "I really never thought about sharing my lover with someone else until I was trying to figure out how to cheer up a friend," or, "I knew she was married so I wasn't even thinking about her and when she approached me I was really surprised," or, "I was dating a couple of guys seriously and thought I was going to have to choose one, but it turned out they knew each other and they were both cool with it."

We are calling this group the accidental polyamorist. Not everyone living a nonmonogamous lifestyle sets out to achieve that status. Sometimes it comes as a big surprise. And often the accidental polyamorist stays poly only for the length of the relationship that got them into poly, although sometimes the experience changes their lives so much they stay poly forever.

Diego was a highly educated twenty-two-year-old immigrant from Mexico when he placed a profile on a well-known dating website. He was trying to find a girlfriend and considered himself monogamous. When he was contacted by a slightly older woman (she was twenty-six) on the site, he was excited to meet her. The first meeting went well, and he was extremely interested in her.

But there was a catch. She explained that she was a married woman with a husband who was encouraging her to explore polyamory. She had been looking through the personals at her husband's urging, and Diego had caught her eye. He had a choice now: say no thanks, or take a risk and try something absolutely new and unthought-of.

He took the chance, started dating her, and let her take him home to meet her husband, a man twenty years older than his wife. The two men got along famously. After a few months of dating, they invited him to move in and become a triad with them. As of this writing, the triad has been together for ten years and is still going strong. Diego wasn't looking for polyamory, but when it found him, he was very happy.

Jim, on the other hand, is in his late sixties and has known about polyamory for years. He just never considered himself poly; instead, he characterizes himself as a "lifestyler"—that is, a recreational swinger. He was very happy as a single man in the swing scene with lots of friends and several occasional lovers. Then one day he met Carol and included her in his circle of friends.

Over the next few months, he and Carol, a married woman with a husband who didn't swing, got together several times. Eventually he realized that he was developing feelings for Carol and let her know that. The solution? Carol introduced him to her husband (who had known about Jim all along and approved of her activities). Jim surprised himself by developing a fast friendship with Carol's husband and now considers himself as being in a triad with the two of them. If this relationship runs its course and someday ends, will Jim still consider himself poly? No. That is not how he sees himself. He sees himself as a lifestyler.

And what about the sociologists and sexologists who study polyamory? Their reasons for being interested in this lifestyle run the gamut.

Dr. Deborah Anapol was frankly interested in nonmonogamy as a personal extension of her life. She writes in her books that she knew that monogamy was not for her, and she went back to school and got her doctorate in clinical psychology partly to allow her to study and more effectively communicate the benefits of having multiple loves in a person's life. Similarly, Dr. Elisabeth Sheff writes in *The Polyamorists Next Door* that she experimented with nonmonogamy in her own life before deciding that while this love style was not personally for her, it was valid for some people and deserved study.

Anthropologist Kikue Fukami received a grant from her university to come to the United States to study American polyamory and complete her doctoral project. She had previously studied marriage strategies in Asia and Europe and felt polyamory represented a good way of approaching family building. But she too had a personal reason for choosing to study what Americans were doing: She wanted to bring that information back to the Japanese people so they could make their own choices. Why?

It turns out that in Japanese culture sometimes a man will have a "second wife" and perhaps an entire second family. The wife and second wife may even know each other, possibly even be friends, but—and it is a big but—in Japan the second wife has no status. All status accrues to the first wife and children, and the second family is rarely acknowledged at all. Fukami felt there had to be better options in building families.

Fukami returned home, completed her doctoral thesis, and then published a popular book about polyamory.[10] She currently has written a play about polyamory and created a board game teaching the concepts of poly. She is making a real effort to introduce these concepts to Japanese culture.

4

The Beginning of Synergy, 1971

Synergy (noun): the interaction or cooperation of two or more organizations, substances, or other agents to produce a combined effect greater than the sum of their separate effects.[1]

In the late 1960s, and early 1970s, many utopian groups were forming, or at least attempting to form, advocating everything from urban group living, back-to-nature farming, and economic co-op trade and bartering, to Israeli kibbutzim–style total property sharing. Many included freeform experimental sexual pairing styles. The organization Family Synergy came into existence during this time, partly because two couples managed to meet.

Chayim (name has been changed for privacy by request of the family), an engineer in the bustling technical world of aerospace, had a family, a satisfying job, and a desire to further enrich his life. He was looking for something quite specific but hard to define. He was not looking to join a commune, make a political statement about planetary resources, or create a model for cooperative living—others were already doing that.

He was actually inspired by the utopian novels of Robert Rimmer: *The Harad Experiment, Proposition Thirty One,* and *InSix.* Rimmer proposed that a group marriage, built by couples who found other couples and married them, could be a powerful and joyful lifestyle. Chayim wondered if this could possibly be true and went on a quest to find out.

After attending meetings put on by numerous groups, he realized he was looking for something else. Instead of looking for ways to change the world, he was looking for ways to enrich his life and the lives of those he cared about. And this turned out to be a key concept that would inspire and infuse the organization he helped found with a purpose that spanned decades.

"In those days it was very hard to meet people," Chayim says. "The only way to contact other like-minded people was to put an ad in the *LA Free Press* and wait for someone to answer it, or answer someone else's ad."[2]

Eventually, after answering a large number of ads and putting in one of their own, they met Pat and Ann Lafollette. Chayim remembers, "We met each other; we liked each other. In fact, Pat and I got along fabulously well." Although they were younger and did not yet have children, the Lafollettes had also read Rimmer's novels and were wondering if group marriage, based on couples, could work.

Pat already had an extraordinary background that would prove beneficial in shaping the philosophies of the new organization. He was a trained scientist, a biologist, and had also earned a degree in sociology. He had lived as a hippie in San Francisco and was a participant in the Summer of Love.

At the time Pat met Chayim, he was working as an artist, making a name for himself in the world of avant-garde art, while his wife used her degree in library science to support them as a research librarian. He understood the concept of intentional community from the inside out.

A deep friendship developed. It became clear that although they were looking for the same thing, the two couples were not quite the right mix to build a marriage together. Instead, they went as a foursome to several discussion groups on communes.

About that adventure, Chayim states, "We blew people away because all they wanted to talk about is who takes out the garbage, or how to *decide* who takes out the garbage—and we wanted to talk about being in a place where people cared about each other. The reason for being there was not political or economic, it was to live with someone you cared for. . . . We ended up getting attacked a lot, because our views were so dissimilar to those of the rest of the room."

They were so dismayed by the responses they were getting, they decided to put an ad of their own in the paper, advertising a meeting to discuss the philosophies of Robert Rimmer. The meeting drew a group of more than a dozen people and was supposed to be about three hours long. But the idea caught fire. At the end of the discussion period, no one was ready to leave, so they adjourned to a local restaurant for dinner and returned to continue the discussion.

Sometime late in the evening they decided that they should do more than just talk about Rimmer's ideas; it was time to *do* something with them. They formed a body called the steering committee, composed of everyone who was at the meeting, and resolved to build an organization to see if these ideas would work in the real world. The new group had no name, a problem that would need a solution sooner than they realized.

One of the new steering committee members mentioned that Rimmer himself would be coming to the Los Angeles area the following month to give a talk at a convention. He proposed they attend the convention to hear Rimmer speak—and to advertise their existence to other like-minded people.

Now came the problem: they had a group, but what to call it? In trying to define what they were looking for, Pat and Chayim often stated they were looking to build a "synergy" in their lives: creating stronger, more vital relationships based on their marriages and providing a stronger family experience for the adults *and* the children.

The steering committee came to the realization that they were talking about family. Obviously, the organization should be called Family Synergy. Later they would invent the term *expanded family* to denote those adults and children that individuals spent a lot of time with and did family activities with: who were family but did not happen to be related by blood or by law.

Several members of the newly formed organization attended the convention the following month and met Robert Rimmer. They found a way to get invited onstage with Rimmer and made their announcement. Pat recalls, "At that time I was a professional artist and had a huge artist's loft in the skid row area of Los Angeles. It was four or five thousand feet. We held the next meeting there just in case we got a good turnout." In fact, fifty or sixty people showed up—and Family Synergy was in business.

"The organization never had a formal structure in the early days," says Pat. "We continued with the steering committee concept. Anybody who was willing to put in the work of keeping Synergy going was automatically on the steering committee. The only people who got to vote on what Synergy would do were the people who put in the work. That system, adopted from other utopian groups of the same period, worked really well for many years."

The system did have its challenges, though. One of the key factors in making the organization work was a concept lifted whole cloth from the way the Quakers operate. The word was *consensus.* Pat says,

> When decisions had to be made, everyone got their say and everyone had to agree before we went forward. Some meetings lasted many long hours while one person was being brought around to the majority view, or at least would eventually say, "Okay, let's give it a try and see how it works."
>
> We kept it this way until the mid or late eighties before . . . enough people started demanding a more rigid structure. Eventually Synergy developed bylaws,

elected positions, all that stuff. I never noticed the organization functioning better because of it.

People kept coming to the meetings, which came to be held monthly. Family Synergy proved to be an enduring organization, partly because of the era and the ideas, but mostly, Pat believes, because of its structure. They never intended to grow the group into a national organization, but people kept getting involved and that turned out to be what people wanted.

"We would get people driving in from San Bernardino County"—a community about fifty miles from Los Angeles—says Pat, "and they would complain about how far they had to come. So we'd say, 'Start your own chapter,' and they would." After that, attendees started groups in Orange County, San Diego, Boston, Delaware Valley (Baltimore/Washington DC area), and elsewhere.

Pat recalls, "The only requirement we had for someone to start a Synergy chapter was they already had to be members of Family Synergy, and that was a requirement that was really unenforceable. The only money we collected from the chapters was dues to help pay for the newsletter."

By the early 1980s there were more than two dozen Family Synergy–inspired groups around the continental United States, with branches in Canada, England, Scotland, Australia, and New Zealand.

Remember that the original goals of Family Synergy were to discuss the possibilities of group marriage based on already married couples coming together with other couples, how to grow those group marriages, and how to sustain them. After a year or two the group began to wonder if they were doing something wrong. No group marriages had formed from the group, and they hadn't heard of any forming anywhere else, either. But something interesting was happening, and it was quite unexpected: a number of people started joining the group who were already in committed long-term relationships—but they weren't built from four people, they were built from three.

Chayim recalls, "We started off advocating group marriages built from two couples or multiple couples . . . we had never thought of triads, it was a totally new idea. Over time we moved to the concept that any kind of multiply committed relationship was okay."

No group marriages based on couples ever formed in Family Synergy and survived. In all the cases that Pat and the authors are aware of, every four-person live-in marriage eventually turned into a triad or fractured further. Even though a four-person marriage composed of two couples that had already weathered the strains of building a stable relationship was doable in theory, as proposed by Rimmer, in the real world this relationship configuration was highly unstable. The collapse of these foursomes almost always happened in less than a year.

Sometimes one of the original four would decide it was not for them and exit the relationship, leaving behind three people, who very often were able to make it a stable triad. Or the four-person marriage fractured further, back to two couples, sometimes with the original partners and sometimes with the partners swapping. And sometimes the effort completely dissolved, with all parties going their separate ways.

These experiences are also reflected in Dr. Deborah Anapol's data on relationship patterns. Anapol agrees with the observations of Pat. She devotes several pages to the formation of triads in her seminal work on multiply committed relationships, *Polyamory: The New Love without Limits.* She concludes that triads, a group relationship built of three people committed to each other, eventually emerge over time as a very stable configuration. There was no theoretical basis explaining the power of the triadic structure to be stable when it was first noticed, but it remains a dominant configuration for polyamorous committed relationships to this day.

The Lafollettes eventually added a third person to their marriage, becoming a happy triad. Pat and Ann Lafollette's third was Joe Hoffman, a man who became, in all senses of the word, their co-husband. Their triad lasted more than fourteen years, which is right in line with the 2009 US Census Bureau data showing around 55 percent of all American marriages lasting fifteen years, although less than a third of marriages get to twenty.

The process of adding a third person to an already existing couple is unique for everybody involved but is particularly fraught for the third person. In 1972, there were no road maps to success in building loving triads, and Joe had many doubts and worries along the way. He wrote a very moving account of his journey to creating his triadic marriage in an issue of the Synergy newsletter. It has been reprinted in the appendix in the back of this book and is well worth the read.

The Lafollette family triad produced and raised two children. By Ann's choice, she had one child from each father. The triad dissolved after fourteen years, with Ann continuing as a couple with Joe instead of with her original husband Pat. However, everyone remained close friends and continued to take their parental duties seriously.

As a case in point, a few years later one of the children got married. Both of the fathers attended the wedding and were honored for their role as father. Most of the attendees had no idea which one was the "bio dad"—and it didn't matter. In 2022, when we reached out to Joe for permission to reprint his Family Synergy article, we were delighted to find out that Joe and Ann were still together in a relationship that has endured.

On reflection, Pat and Ann were not consciously looking for a man to join their marriages and were modestly surprised at how their lives turned out. One of the enduring fantasies for many American men of this era, especially men who identified as straight (or heterosexual in the parlance of the 1970s), was to have two women, two wives to call their own.

And yet we will go out on a limb and state that in their experience, there certainly seem to be more two-men/one-woman triads in the alternative loving community than two-women/one-man. If there is an explanation for this, we have never heard one proposed. One possible theory is that there are simply more men than women involved and available in these communities, and therefore numbers alone would favor the formation of two-men/one-woman triads.

WHAT FAMILY SYNERGY DID

The Family Synergy Newsletter

As volunteer-run social groups learn very quickly, a consistently published newsletter is essential to creating the experience of community. The Synergy newsletter was the glue that held hundreds, and eventually thousands, of people together.

Not only did the newsletter announce events (remember, this was pre-internet communication, and almost before privately owned computers of any sort), it published articles by members giving advice on every topic under the sun concerning multiply committed relationships. People chronicled their joys and sorrows, successes and failures, in the adventures of expanded family and expanded loves.

One series of articles was by the Lafollette triad. They talked about their emotional journeys in creating their group marriage and the factors that went into their huge decision to all have children together, including Ann's choice to have one child by each of her husbands, and especially what that meant to Joe, their third!

Monthly Meetings

The monthly meetings were originally general topic presentations or group discussions about aspects of group marriage, and sometimes included special interest presentations on topics such as how to put together a group household or plan a commune.

Pat remembers,

On the first anniversary, we noted that not a single group marriage had formed among our members. The steering committee had a soul-searching discussion of what we were doing wrong. We noted that the complexities of daily life, work, economics, and geography were an effective barrier to the formation of residential group marriages.

The conclusion was that we needed to broaden our purpose from group marriage itself to the process by which members might get there, and other types of interpersonal relationships that might be alternatives to residential group marriage or be stepping-stones on the way. I suggested the idea that the more possibilities one is open to, the more likely one (or more) of them will actually come about.

This marked a major shift in focus for the organization. Programs and workshops now focused on issues such as jealousy, possessiveness, control, communication, and adopting a friendship-based model for loving relationships instead of the current (from the Victorian to the 1950s) ideal of "romantic love." Internally they referred to these programs as GIT, for Get It Together. In some ways the classes were wildly successful.

Chayim and Pat colead the jealousy and interpersonal communications workshops, designed for six to eight couples. Here they grappled with the basics, like how to handle the emotions of jealousy or the feeling of being displaced temporarily from the primary position by a spouse's newer lover, sometimes referred to as NRE, or new relationship energy.

Some programs dealt with how to schedule time. The ability to love may be limitless, but there are only so many hours in a week. People have to decide: Who gets Friday night, spouse or lover? Also, who you are spending Thanksgiving, Christmas, Hanukkah, or New Year's Eve with? Being sensitive and learning what day is special to each person, turns out to be a critical skill.

These issues have more impact on a relationship where one, or all, of the other partners are nonresidential or otherwise not considered a part of the family. One brilliant result of Synergy's expanded family concept is that you don't have to separate from your spouse to share a holiday with your lover; if everyone is happy and comfortable with each other, you can share the special times together.

And what about what to tell the children—and when? This is an enduring question for every parent in an alternative lifestyle. In fact, this may be a universal question because a parent in every type of dating situation faces this. Many single parents today have to decide when, and if, to tell their children about a new person in the parent's life. We believe honesty is always the best policy, making allowances for age appropriateness in presenting the information.

Lynn, a successful lawyer living in Beverly Hills, and his wife, Phyllis, an accountant and mother of their two children, were Family Synergy members who tried the traditional Robert Rimmer paradigm of building a four-person nonresidential marriage with another couple who, in this case, were childless. After a few months, the man in the other couple dropped out of the relationship but Anne stayed.

Phoenix is the name they chose for their triad when Anne moved in as their live-in third. Originally, they tried to pretend Anne had moved in simply as a roommate: a renter, as it were. They thought they had successfully hidden their relationship from their fourteen-year-old son, Andrew.

He laughed when they eventually discussed it with him and asked if they thought he was blind! He could certainly see that the way Anne treated his father and mother was not strictly friendship. And what's more—he approved! He didn't think his parents had ever been happier.

Phoenix would last for twenty-five years as a triad, and the three considered themselves a true marriage. After the death of Lynn, Phyllis and Anne remained together until Phyllis died some ten years later.

Coauthor Terry Lee Brussel-Rogers is a mother of two, as well as a relationship/life coach and a clinical hypnotherapist. She lectures on the benefits of polyamory and sometimes uses the example of Lynn and Phyllis to point out that children are very intuitive, something the adults in Family Synergy would discover over and over again.

She has a personal story as well:

> My daughter discovered our lifestyle when at age five she walked into the guest room to find Grace cuddling with Daddy. When she came to our bedroom to tell me, she found Grace's husband, Roy, and I cuddling. I explained that Mommy and Daddy loved each other and also loved Roy and Grace, who had been family by choice for several months at this point. I made the explanation very simple and matter of fact. We were spending a lot of time together, sharing everything from trips to the zoo, evening dinners, holidays, and birthdays together, so the children were very comfortable with them. Although not a live-in situation, we were family.

Remember we mentioned GIT? As Pat explains it, after a year of meetings where expectations were high that just by coming together and spending time talking about it, group marriages would start to form, Family Synergy realized it needed to be doing more to help people. A series of classes, talks, and seminars was launched teaching the concepts of communication, jealousy, group household building, and bonding. Much later, at the culmination of these classes, a group of Synergy members formed GIT One. They spent months planning and working on the formation of an intentional rural commune. They pooled resources, bought land, and moved there. The commune stayed in operation for about three years.

Outreach was an aggressive priority in the early years of Synergy. Pat Lafollette estimates that he was invited to speak more than a thousand times on college campuses during the first ten years of Synergy's existence, by both teachers and student groups. He also routinely traveled around the country to speak at the meetings of other, similar alternative lifestyle organizations.

Terry remembers that Chayim had his own "outreach" specialty. He would go to swing clubs, usually with another Synergy member, like Terry, and talk with the swingers about the advantages and joys of committed multiple relationships. He reasoned that swingers, who had already opened up their relationships in a very controlled and limited fashion, were fertile minds to convert to the ideas of true emotionally open relationships.

"He would spend the entire evening in the living room talking and handing out Synergy flyers," Terry recalls, "never getting to the bedrooms, but ready to buttonhole the next couple as they walked back into the living room."

Throughout the years, Synergy held many types of events. One of the best attended was the annual convention. In the early years, the convention might be a camping trip in the San Bernardino Mountains to places like Camp de Benneville Pines, which allowed clothing-optional camping if Synergy booked the whole camp. In later years, the annual conventions tended to take place in a hotel.

The monthly barbeques hosted by Synergy members in their homes have a special place in Pat Lafollette's heart. "Of all the events that Family Synergy hosted, these always felt like just getting together with family," he says. And that was the most important thing for him—the building of intentional and expanded families, the sense of community, fun events like backyard barbeques, picnics, and going camping together. All human beings are social; this kind of connection is a vital part of being human.

Synergy also threw its own adult-only "permissive parties," which became ever more popular as the years went by and in a peculiar way may have contributed to the eventual decline of the organization. (More on that later in the chapter.)

SOME INDIVIDUAL STORIES
FROM THE EARLY YEARS

Casey's Story (A Family Synergy Member Interviewed in 2014)

The year was 1974. Casey (names changed at her request) remembers herself as a somewhat shy person, but at age twenty-five, she was still as adventurous as her friends. She had been going with a boyfriend to Elysium Fields, a clothing-optional club and resort in Topanga Canyon, and she started to notice the other naked women more than she thought she would.

"After a little while I began to think I might be bisexual," she recalls, "and so my boyfriend and I talked about having a threesome with another woman."

The boyfriend had learned about Family Synergy, which by now was welcoming anyone who thought they might have an interest in building any type of multiply committed relationship, and took her to a meeting. She found the people incredibly welcoming and open-minded. The couple began attending as many of the events as they could.

It didn't take long before she had her first girlfriend. "Actually, I did not bring her home to my boyfriend to have a threesome." She smiles at the memory. "I never did bring her to him; I kept her to myself. Of course, I kept my boyfriend, too."

Casey made many friends and collected a few additional lovers, too. She spent our interview reminiscing about some of the strange entanglements a person can get into in a loving and permissive environment, where the rules are still being invented. She remembers two couples who got into a crossed-communication and mixed-message situation, exacerbated by unmet expectations. And, as good stories must have, there is a twist.

I had a lover named Justin who I sometimes slept with, and he had a wife, Betty. This particular weekend they were at a Family Synergy campout and were spending time with another couple they knew well, a very prominent couple in the group, Herman and Sue. Betty chose to sleep that night with Herman, which left Sue's bed empty unless Justin would sleep with her—which he agreed to do.

Ah, but there was a rub. As Casey tells it, when Justin, who was a curmudgeonly kind of person anyway, got to Sue's bed, he said he was too tired to have sex with her and just wanted to sleep. Sue was livid, and she made sure everyone heard about it. Casey's recollection of her point was, "Hey, if you were sleeping with your own wife, I would be sleeping with my husband and getting sex. Instead, your wife is getting my sex!"

Talk about role reversal. How many men have tried to get away with the "not tonight dear, I have a headache" routine—and with somebody else's wife, to boot?

Did Family Synergy have an enduring impact on Casey's life? "Oh yes. I found my first husband, Charles, at a Family Synergy event. We were so in love with each other we practically eloped, and then later our friends planned a formal wedding for us."

One of those friends was a man named Dan. At the time he was just a friend, but after Charles moved Casey to a little town ninety miles away to follow his career, it became natural for Casey to stay at Dan's when she was in town visiting friends and relatives.

"It took quite some time, but eventually we got closer and closer." Casey asked her husband if he was okay with her going to bed with Dan, and he said yes. When she asked if he wanted to know about it, he was more uncomfortable; he finally said he did not want to be told if she and Dan started having sex. However, there may be something to psychic intuition. Casey did go to bed with Dan—and fifteen minutes after they finished having sex, her husband called to see how she was doing. "Dan and I were laughing so hard during the call, it didn't take long for Charles to figure out that something was up."

Her marriage to Charles did not last, but she remained friends with him for life. And as for Dan? After her marriage ended, she and Dan remained lovers—eventually primary partners—and ultimately married. They remained together until his death in 2014.

Terry's Story

Terry became aware of Family Synergy in 1975 in what was at that time a very traditional way: by personal contact that was totally accidental.

My first husband, Richard, and I learned of Family Synergy from a couple named Chet and Vickey. Vickey answered an ad I had in the *Free Press* for a babysitter. By that time, I had been reading the science fiction novels of Robert Heinlein, Robert Rimmer, and others for many years. The characters in them had open multiply committed relationships, and I already had an open marriage with my husband, but except for a small circle of friends I just didn't know of very many people who were living this lifestyle.

Vickey turned out to be as involved with Robert A. Heinlein's *Stranger in a Strange Land* as I was. We talked for two hours and had practically planned our lives together before our husbands got home from work. Vickey was the first woman I ever saw make love to my husband. Chet did have most of my attention at the time.

We did not stay together for long, because despite everything else we had in common, they were not into making the kind of calendared time commitments or the long-range plans Richard and I believed were necessary to any relationship. They did make a lasting difference in our lives, though, by introducing us to Family Synergy. Suddenly we were not just oddballs who thought we could actually live the lifestyles outlined in Heinlein's novels; we were members of a wide community of kindred spirits who had a similar philosophy, many of them with a lot more real-life experience with open committed relationships than we did and who were willing to help us learn what worked and what did not. Synergy became such an important part of my own identity, I spent the next ten years devoting much of my spare time to promoting and doing outreach for the organization. Eventually I became a board member.

BENEFITS TO CHILDREN OF EXPANDED FAMILIES

What about children in Synergy? After all the name of the organization is *Family* Synergy. One of the basic tenets of the organization was always that it existed to help adults grapple with how they could build relationships and community with other adults, but one of the major reasons to go to so much effort was to create relationships that benefited everyone—and that meant the children, too.

Terry observes that one of the many advantages of having an expanded family is the inclusion of more caring adults in a child's everyday life. Having more adults with unique skill sets taking an interest in the children's welfare can really be great assistance to the parents. At one point, Terry's expanded family included a poet, a gourmet cook, and a child educator. Talk about a broad base for the children to learn from!

Because children were a primary focus in the early days of Family Synergy, several events were held each year that adults could bring their children to. One of those was the annual convention at Camp de Benneville Pines. One of the authors (Glen) attended a campout there in about 1978 and had several illuminating conversations with both adults and children about their experiences in Family Synergy.

It was a weekend filled with picnics and hikes, campfire sing-alongs, games for adults and children, and community dinners. If two or more adults disappeared into the cabins for some special alone time with each other, well there were plenty of adults around to supervise the children adequately.

Does this mean the children didn't know what their parents were doing? Hardly. As every parent knows, by the time a child reaches eleven or twelve, you're not fooling them about anything. Most of the children were between eight and fifteen years old and seemed to be happy kids having a good time.

But two things stand out in Glen's memory. The children who were between twelve and fifteen were very body conscious, working hard to stay covered up. Some of them didn't want to go swimming because they wanted to wear more than just swimsuits. And they were very vocal in expressing their opinions about what their parents were doing. All of them liked having extra adults in their lives to take them to the movies or the store or help with homework. All of them thought their parents were weird. One fourteen-year-old assured me that when she finally had a boyfriend, she was going to be monogamous, because she didn't want to have confusing relationships like her parents had.

The parents, of course, knew about the body shyness of their children and the dogmatic attitudes toward "conventional" morality expressed by some of their children. They shrugged and explained it as "children always have to have something to rebel about, to set themselves apart from the parents." The common belief among the parents seemed to be, "We've shown them there is more than one choice in the world, and someday they may decide open relationships are a surprisingly good way to live your life."

And before we mark it down as an aberration of 1970s kids in rebellion against their hippie parents, we remind you Family Synergy was never a hippie movement, Pat Lafollette notwithstanding. Most of the people in the group at this time were in their late twenties or thirties with careers and fairly long-term marriages.

SO WHAT ULTIMATELY HAPPENED TO FAMILY SYNERGY?

Even as early as 1974, Family Synergy started seriously tracking the demographic makeup of its members and talking about what it meant. The average age of the membership when Family Synergy started was around thirty years old. In other words, Family Synergy appealed to young families that had been established for a while and were raising young children but still had a pioneering spirit about relationships.

For a short time in the mid-1970s, the average age of members joining Family Synergy actually dropped to the mid-twenties. Shortly after the realization set in that the original Rimmer model of building group marriages out of existing couples was not practical or possible for most people, the organization started welcoming the many people who were experimenting with other forms of intimate connection. It turned out that there were people interested in joining who were building triads or choosing to have extra lovers outside of their primary relationships that they never intended to turn into group marriage.

This was the era when Terry found Synergy. She was a young mother and wife, only twenty-two years old, when she became one of the youngest Family Synergy members ever.

During the 1980s, the average age of the membership started rising. Fewer people with small children joined, and eventually the typical member was either a single person with no children or a couple with grown children. Family Synergy had unintentionally shifted away from its original mandate simply because the people who joined were more often individuals looking for community rather than families looking for community.

As we said before, this was not a surprise to the leadership. Remember that the original goal of Family Synergy was to discuss the possibilities of group marriage based on already married couples coming together with other couples, how to grow those group marriages, and how to sustain them.

Commentary about this trend appeared many times in the Family Synergy newsletter, along with soul-searching articles asking if the organization was becoming obsolete or losing its mandate. Members proposed many strategies for additional outreach and membership drives. It was during this period that Terry worked tirelessly to promote Family Synergy to interested younger people, hosting many child-friendly events like the family picnics of the decade before.

But with Synergy's open-door policy of welcoming everyone who was interested in the philosophies of open committed relationships, there was no real way to exclude people because of their age—and it would have been anathema to the philosophies of inclusion to have done so.

By the early 1990s, the shift in priorities was complete. Around this time, Family Synergy chose to make a full reciprocity agreement with an organization called the Olympians, a traveling nudist group. (Some nudist organizations owned their own ranches or facilities; others met in members' homes or rented facilities for their events.) The Olympians shared some of Family Synergy's original values, but the group was really based on swinging values. The average age of the Olympians was over fifty, and many members were sixty-five years old or older.

Overnight, the average age in Family Synergy shifted dramatically higher. Younger people interested in the original philosophies of Family Synergy were increasingly uncomfortable in the new group. Fewer and fewer joined. Outreach decreased during this time, and the number of events fell dramatically. There were no child-friendly events taking place anymore. Most of the monthly events became adult-only "permissive parties," and attendance at the yearly convention plummeted.

In the mid-2000s, Terry took a look at the issues facing Family Synergy and tried to reinfuse the organization with the fire and vision of the original founders. She was the keynote speaker at the 2006 Family Synergy Annual Convention. A portion of her keynote address seems a fitting wrap-up and reminder of the things that made Family Synergy great:

> Hello everyone, happy to see you all today. I am Terry Brussel-Gibbons, a longtime member. I joined in 1975 and am a current board member of Family Synergy. I would like to address this talk to the value Family Synergy has had in my life—and the lives of all of us here. I raised two children in an open marriage

which included intimate friendships with people who were like family to our children as well.

I believed when I started raising my children that a larger family would create an environment for better-adjusted and thinking children. My children were exposed to multiple perspectives. They learned that not every adult sees things the same way. They developed an instinctive openness to new ideas. Also, they watched and learned by observation the ways adults negotiate with each other, the give and the take of communication in an expanded family, which in some ways took the place for us of the old extended family—the non-nuclear family, with uncles, aunts, and grand, great grandparents, tribes, and clans.

Why is there such a need for "expanded" families as pioneered by Family Synergy in the 1970s?

The breakup of community to sell more products was promoted by commercial media just after World War II. After all, a large family living under one roof needs fewer refrigerators, cars and washing machines than do two or three nuclear families living in separate apartments. Many of Synergy's original members were the children of parents who saw this happen and may have had some regrets about it. Nuclear families may be great for business, but a natural hunger was created by this movement away from the larger expanded family. There was an empty feeling of not belonging, sometimes filled in by religious cults, and -isms. We humans were created needing family.

Where did Synergy come into it for me? I joined when I was twenty-two. I came from a small family and craved a much larger one. My water brothers in high school were my first family-by-choice. Family Synergy, *an intentional community*, helped fill this need for me as a young wife and mother. It showed me my first functioning group home—the Allot House—and through one of its members I was introduced to my first child-centered commune, adults who raised their children together in a large home with plenty of loving interaction. Synergy became very central to my life as I put in volunteer time coordinating the annual Passover Seder, which Chayim led for many years. I was on the board for five years and even managed to attend board meetings by telephone when I was on a camping trip in Yosemite before cell phones, shivering in a phone booth—okay, I was a little compulsive about it.

In those early days, Synergy gave me a choice of kindred spirits to love, in bed and out, people who understood that it was possible to love and be committed to more than one significant other. I was able to meet people who were actually living in the triads and group marriages I had read about in [science fiction] books, to learn that this lifestyle really was possible. I learned that one could be happily married and still have a joyous committed secondary relationship which could last through many years. I've been blessed with relationships which have lasted over a quarter of a century, which started in those Synergy years. I met my husband, Paul, through Family Synergy, and also Marcus, the third in our residential triad, who came to us in 2000 through the first Family Synergy meeting to be held at our home in many years.

Today I am in a four-way group marriage with my legal husband, Paul, and our handfasted partners Marcus and Laura. We live in a lovely home with two of our other water brothers—Carl and Will. Carl was also an old-time Synergy member, while Will came to us through Live the Dream. He is a writer of columns and novels on the poly lifestyle.

These special people who are part of my life give my grandchildren extra grandparents, aunts, and uncles—role models and people who care about them.

Synergy was important in the '70s and '80s to a lot of people when there were far fewer choices of poly groups to relate to. Even as more groups were formed, it still offered a feeling of continuity and closeness with people who had known each other, helped each other in times of crisis, shared the good times, and watched each other's children grow up.

The last board meeting I attended a couple of months ago had a dichotomy of people: those currently involved in Synergy, many of them for five years or less, and several old-timers from the '70 s and '80s, who, like me, came out of the woodwork to save something which had been very important to them at one time.

I'd like to focus now on why Synergy shrunk from a membership of over a thousand at its high point in the '70s to one of less than a hundred today and how we can grow it back to a higher level. People want what you want! If we focus on what it is that is special to us about Synergy today and what we loved in the past, we will be able to find the passion that we need to grow again.

Ask yourself, why did you join Family Synergy? What you see here is what Synergy still has to offer its members and those who may become members in the future. What do we get out of polyamory? First, Personal Growth: Issues are quickly brought forth—consider it a trial by fire; once you have gone through it, your relationship is stronger, and you become better at resolving issues. Some will do it without tools of communication (and often fail) but there is a hunger to find ways of dealing with jealousy, money, time, and territory.

Polyamory provides the answer to this hunger through support groups such as Family Synergy, Live the Dream, and Loving More. Tools, modeling, and resources are available. Some examples of tools which have helped us include poly counselors, using formatted discussions such as active listening and nonviolent communication. Hypnosis, as demonstrated by the workshop I gave earlier today, has its place among the tools we offer those who come to our meetings.

Sexual joy: All else being said, the sex provided by groups like ours is great. New relationship chemistry and observation of techniques brought in by new partners and experiences add to the mix. The presence of multiple partners encourages poly couples, triads, and more to live the concepts that love, like bread, must be freshly baked each day to stay delicious. Humans need touch, personal validation, accountability, and community. Polyamory excels here also.

Interestingly enough, the divorce rate among those in open relationships is lower than that of the general population. Significantly lower according to some research.

Spirituality: Sex metaphysically connects the participants to sharing soul consciousness free of guilt. Morality as practiced throughout much of our history generated guilt and was used against people to control them. Real spiritual awareness unifies the mind, body, and spirit. The Tantric path is one example. HAI, the Human Awareness Institute is another path.

My personal choice is to be a Judeo-Pagan. Church of All Worlds, based on *Stranger in a Strange Land*, was the first legally recognized Neo-Pagan religion in the United States. According to Pagan tradition, the Goddess tells her children in our Earth that "all acts of love and pleasure are my rituals." What could be more poly than that? Sex is integrated into the family synergy of a poly family.

Human survival: If the Serbs and the Croatians were getting together in sensitivity groups and having sensual closeness, what chance would there be of them having sectarian fighting? What for? Soul sharing creates closeness; we humans were designed to bond through sex.

Jealousy can be an extremely destructive force. Jealousy is an emotion caused by worry, boundary violation, and fear of loss. Polyamory and groups such as Family Synergy provide another way of living that can work. Love choices are important! If much of the population is as nonmonogamous as the Kinsey Reports show, there are a lot of needs that go unfilled. I would not choose the chancy situation of a marriage which could be destroyed by my husband finding me in bed with a loved one. If my husband finds me in such a situation, he joins me there. Millions of lives are ruined by divorce. Here we can and must help.

Nationalism can be a destructive force: Polyamory can be a force for promotion of tolerance and acceptance. We humans can't make war without limits like we did in the past. An almost universal technique of warfare has been to deny the enemy access to infrastructure. That this will never work in an enclosed environment such as a generation ship or space station is obvious, but as our weapons have become so powerful and do permanent harm to the environment, the Earth has become our space station.

Our spaceship Earth can become a radioactive example of the folly of state-driven politics and policies. Human awareness of the beauty and value of life can find expression beyond the borders of individual countries. Polyamory may well be a necessary tool for human survival if we don't want our grandchildren to glow in the dark.

Lovers make better neighbors. A society that allows love will find common ground beyond the limits imposed by culture, religion, and nationalism. In fact, the very human urge to see what making love to someone who is from another culture is like, helps demonstrate that we all *can* get along.

There are many poly-oriented groups today, all fighting for new membership and to maintain the membership they have. This is generally not because anyone is making money on these groups. It is because they want a way to meet with people they can relate to, find family, sexual love, companionship, and all these things we have written on the board here. We could all actually accomplish this purpose more effectively by being inclusive rather than exclusive. Isn't that what all this is about?

So let's go out and bring what Synergy has to the people who can delight in it![3]

The keynote address was well received, and the entire annual convention had a note of optimism about it. A new outreach program was initiated, and Family Synergy began having events again on a monthly or bimonthly basis. These events were often put together by Terry, who took on the job of events coordinator. During the period between 2006 and 2011, many of Synergy's in-person events were hosted in coordination with Synergy's kindred organization, Live the Dream.

In 2011 Synergy held its Fortieth Anniversary Convention and Annual Business Meeting at a nudist resort called Treehouse. The event was fairly well attended thanks to the tireless efforts of a few volunteers who kept outreach going. Terry was the events coordinator for the convention and heavily promoted it to many of the poly organizations in the area. She also presented several of the convention's events.

All this time, Synergy had continued to struggle with low membership and low turnout at its events. The governing board was primed to take up a new proposal at this business meeting. Many of the board members thought that since the two organizations were working so closely together, combining Family Synergy and Live the Dream into one organization made great sense and would be helpful to both. These board members had in mind to ask Terry to take on the job of chairperson of the combined organization.

But politics intervened. A small cadre of old-time members of Family Synergy thought Synergy should stay just the way it was. Some of the people showing up at the business meeting had not been members for years; they had rejoined on the first day of the convention to be able to vote on the issue. They nominated their own person for chair and effectively blocked a vote for merging the organizations. As Terry remembers it, some of them went out of their way to heap personal attacks on her that were so hurtful she withdrew from consideration as chairperson and decided to resign as events coordinator.

The new Synergy leadership never succeeded in filling the events coordinator position left vacant by Terry and lost many of their other volunteers as well. Without dedicated volunteers, it was not possible to sustain the momentum of the organization. Within a few months of its fortieth anniversary, all meetings and activities of Family Synergy had ceased in the Los Angeles area.

A dedicated individual continued to maintain the Family Synergy website for a few more years, but strangely the website never reported on local events, even though much was happening in the Los Angeles area. Live the Dream repeatedly offered calendar events and articles but were refused. The only information that appeared on the website came from Family Tree, an East Coast chapter of the original Synergy. The website went dark by 2018.

Family Synergy lasted more than forty years. It was a leader in the 1970s and 1980s, shaping many of the concepts of present-day polyamory. It touched many people's lives. It survived for decades after its founders were no longer actively involved. It spun off dozens of organizations, like Live the Dream (West Coast) and Family Tree (East Coast), groups that are still active and vital in the polyamory community today. This is quite an achievement for an organization that was never intended to last past a few meetings to explore the concept of group marriage.

5

Morehouse, 1968

It was 1984 when Glen first stumbled across the mention of Morehouse. He was living in the San Francisco Bay area, where his wife was enrolled in a postgraduate degree program in human sexuality at a prestigious private school run by Wardell Pomeroy, a longtime associate of Alfred Kinsey. The school is the Institute for Advanced Study of Human Sexuality, accredited by the Western Accreditation Association to grant master's and doctoral degrees in several disciplines.

Students come to the institute from all around the world to add advanced degrees to their clinical or research résumés. They are anthropologists, sex researchers who may already have reputations in their fields, doctors of medicine or philosophy, and even clergy. This is a serious academic environment—nobody's fooling around with sex; this is the big league.

So when Glen's wife came home laughing about how angry and annoyed her teachers were about the "competition" across the bay, Glen had to ask, "What competition?"

What competition, indeed. A man named Victor Baranco had set up a school—or commune, or radio station, or subversive organization (reports vary)—less than twenty miles away in the little town of Lafayette, and somehow he convinced the State of California to let him grant degrees in human sexuality. And he was a charlatan of the first degree—at least according to some of her school's faculty—and should be shut down immediately.

Glen picks up the narrative:

My wife insisted we perform some fieldwork, get inside the organization and check them out—purely for scientific reasons, of course. She was very amused about her teacher's consternation, but she wanted to know who, or what, was Morehouse?

Like characters in a detective novel, we decided to go in deep undercover. She was not going to admit her association with the institute, and I would pass myself off as a visiting fireman from Los Angeles. We knew this would work. We went ahead and used our real names when we signed up for a Basic Sense course.[1] For professional reasons our last names are different and so we could either admit we knew each other during the course or pretend we did not.

The drive to Lafayette was pleasant and the grounds are well kept at the school (or commune, or whatever it is). The most peculiar thing about the experience so far was the color scheme of the buildings: All six or seven structures on the property were painted purple. As Glen would come to learn, when Morehouse moves in, the buildings turn purple. That actually proves helpful when visiting a Morehouse site in urban areas like downtown San Francisco— just look for the purple house.

About twenty people were gathered in the living room of the largest building on the property when we arrived. Most of them were like us: strangers to each other who were attending a seminar. The presenters were a man and a woman who lived at Morehouse and were advanced students in the arcane technology that Vic Baranco had been inventing (or rediscovering) as he went along.

Our cover lasted just long enough to pay our seminar fees and sit down. In walked another student from my wife's school, who hollered pleasantly, "Hi Ronnie!" and came over to sit down by us. He had been attending courses at Morehouse for months and everybody here knew him. We had a good laugh out of it. Oh well—now we could relax and enjoy the experience.

SO WHO—OR WHAT—IS MOREHOUSE?

Morehouse is not a title, but an enduring nickname that captures one of the cornerstones of the More philosophy. According to Vic, every person is at this very moment perfect—every choice you have made getting to this moment in time has been the right choice for you. There is nothing to fix, repair, improve, or recover from; you are just fine the way you are.

And being perfect, you are perfectly capable of making more choices in your life—in fact you can choose to have as much More in your life as you desire: More fun, More pleasure, More health, More goodies, More relationships . . . you can change whatever you want and choose More if that is your desire!

Many people find starting from this concept of perfection very empowering—and effective in creating change.

The official title that Vic and his wife Suzanne gave this enterprise—which would go on to touch the lives of uncounted thousands, spin off more than seventy satellite Morehouse communes across the nation, be presented in hundreds of private living rooms as Mark Groups over five decades—was the Institute of Human Abilities. Nobody ever uses this name. Ever.

Walking into the Basic Sense course (short for Basic Sensuality, and don't for a moment think the play on words is unintentional) that day, Glen had no idea that this had already been going on for sixteen years. In fact, the Institute of Human Abilities (and now, even we are going to stop using that name) had its beginning in the Barancos' living room in Lafayette, California.

According to Laurie Rivlin Heller, writing in the *Journal of the Communal Studies Association*, "The Institute of Human Abilities was founded in the summer of 1968 by Vic Baranco. By age thirty-four, he had been a success in everything he had attempted in his entire life. He had acquired along the way a loving wife, two perfect children and all the material accoutrements that this society had to offer."[2]

The Barancos lived a normal suburban life for the 1960s. He was a successful used appliance salesman; they owned their own home and raised children. By his own standards, he was an accomplished man. In fact, in an interview he gave in the 1990s that was published on the Morehouse website, Vic described himself as being successful in everything he had ever tried to do.

These successes led him to review deeply what he was doing correctly, so he began formulating his philosophy of abundance and teaching it to interested people in the living room of his own home. The informal meetings at his home became so popular, he took the talk on the road and began speaking in other people's homes.

Finding a number of like-minded people at his Sense talks, he trained them to host and facilitate small discussion groups in their own homes and elsewhere. Called Mark Groups, they were a sensitivity encounter–type experience designed to be presented by people who were not trained therapists or facilitators but who had a good sense of human needs and emotions.

Mark Group experiences were usually set up as a three-to-six-week cycle, and people were asked to attend as many of the meetings in a cycle as they could. The three basic exercises at a Mark Group were: Withholds and Overts, Mirror Dance, and Hot Seat. Vic always charged for attending a Mark Group or seminar course—but there was a catch, which we'll get to shortly. He expected his events to make money. In fact, one of the other basic premises of his philosophy was that making money by providing value to other people was proof that the service given had value.

How's that again? Remember that Heller described Vic as a "used appliance salesman"? Well, the trainers at Morehouse had a much more colorful story to tell about his humble beginnings. In the story Glen was told, Vic Baranco had been a hugely successful used *car* salesman, with all the sleazy connotations that image inspires, when he discovered the More concept.

The mythos told to us at Morehouse in 1984 was that Vic was not just the most successful used car salesman in the world, he was a world-class con artist and a personal friend of Werner Erhard, the inventor of Erhard Seminars Training (EST).

According to the legend, Werner and Vic spent many nights in the early years hanging out together and hammering out their mutual philosophies. Vic insisted that Werner understand that human beings do not, cannot, and will not think something has value if they get it for free. You must charge all the market will bear, and then they will be satisfied. Anyone who attended an EST intensive seminar during the 1970s and 1980s would see this philosophy in action; the seminars had a reputation for being very pricey.

But con artist—doesn't that imply some sort of scam? A swindle where the mark gets suckered in and is separated from their money while thinking they are getting a good deal? Wait a minute—why is it that the encounter groups being held in living rooms all over America are called Mark Groups? In carny language, the "mark" is the customer who is there to be wowed and entertained and painlessly separated from their money. Everybody wins: the carnival stays in business and the mark goes home happy.

It's all coming together. The man has an enormous sense of humor—and a deep street-level understanding of human motivation that could only have developed in a premier salesman. And he is right.

Over the course of many weekends spent at the Lafayette Morehouse site between 1984 and 1987, Glen attended countless seminars and experiences. He watched trainers, using the philosophies developed by Victor Baranco, guide people into new ways of thinking that opened up their sex lives and mental horizons. These experiences truly changed their lives.

We mentioned that Morehouse *always* charged as much for an experience as they could get away with, reasoning that the more people paid, the more they would value the experience. But that is not quite true. In fact, money is just one way of measuring value—and Vic knew it.

No person who came to Morehouse was ever turned away for lack of money. Vic, the con man with a heart of gold, gave out scholarships hand over fist. This meant that the person might pay some small amount or find a way to give back to the community in labor or skills they had. One woman Glen knew moved into the Lafayette compound with her small child, stayed there for a year, and paid not a penny. She donated hours each week watching children and organizing community events like food drives. On the other hand, two medical doctors were in residence during the time Glen was attending seminars at the Lafayette compound. One provided medical services to the residents for his keep; the other had a thriving practice outside and did not want to put any labor into the community. He and his wife simply liked the people so much they moved in to be around the group, and for six months they paid the equivalent daily rate of staying in a three-star hotel. Everyone felt they got good value.

Now, since this is a book on the history of polyamory we should probably ask: Does Morehouse practice polyamory?

Aside from the fact that the term was coined some two decades after Morehouse began, we can just picture sitting in the living room with Vic Baranco and asking him that question. In our imagined conversation he blinks a couple of times and says, quite casually, "I don't care how many people you have sex with. Tell me, how good is the sex you're having?"

How good, indeed. Functionally speaking, sex is an activity that gets better with practice. Add knowledge, stir in a little imagination, learn to focus on your partners' pleasure and your own, and you can have immensely satisfying sex every time—with a partner you've been married to for twenty years or a yummy new partner you've just met.

Morehouse does not espouse a particular philosophy of relationships. It focuses on giving individuals the tools they need to bring what they want into their lives. However, to get these tools into the hands of individuals, the community deals with sex in a very innovative way.

Morehouse in 1984 was both an open and closed community: open because anyone might attend classes, learn the technology, even stay a night or a weekend at one of the houses; closed because (surprise!) there were rules about whom a Morehousian may have sex with.

If you were a resident and were "screened," you were allowed to have sex with any other Morehousian who wanted to be with you, anywhere in the world. If you were not screened, you may not have sex with any of them. Screening developed early on at Morehouse as a way to address the health needs of people who are being deeply intimate with one another.

Screening is quite simple, with a very few rules to follow, and it lets you know immediately who is an insider and who is an outsider. Some communal groups would historically impose arbitrary rules that dictated who a member could or could not have intercourse with; Oneida comes to mind in this regard. Morehouse's decision was to use a much more self-actualized and self-determined method.

Morehouse's system was a health screening, using the most up-to-date scientific information available. The person wishing to be screened submitted to a complete physical with a blood and urine workup to rule out any infectious diseases, with particular emphasis on any sexually transmitted diseases. And then they waited for whatever incubation period was necessary and got tested again.

But that's just the health test. The person undergoing the screening process also agreed to follow one simple rule: they must refrain from any mucus membrane contact or exchange of bodily fluids with anyone until the screening period is over; after the screening period, they were allowed to have mucus membrane contact or exchange of bodily fluids only with other people who have passed screening. That even means no kissing of anyone not screened—not once. None! Not even family members, including your great Aunt Hattie who hasn't had sex since her flapper days, was allowed to kiss you on the mouth.

This turned out to be a powerful winnowing device. Once screened, a person potentially had a choice of hundreds of sex partners, including people who had studied sexual pleasure for years. All you had to do was promise to never make mucus membrane contact or share bodily fluids with anyone outside the screen.

It proved impossible to do for some people. Someone who broke screening was expected to admit it and immediately cease intimate contact with all other members of the tribe. They might be called on publicly to explain why they broke the screen and would be closely questioned as to their motivations and desires: Did they still want to be part of the community, or were they opting out?

If the person wanted to return to the sexual community, they had to go through screening again—and the waiting period depended on the judgment of the medical person administering the tests. All the time they are waiting they are missing out on the intimacies everyone else is getting. Most people didn't break the screen twice, unless they decided it is time for them to move on.

MOREHOUSE TODAY

The original Morehouse campus at Lafayette, California, with room for two hundred residents, has been in continuous operation for more than fifty years. Morehouse Oakland, a stately old Victorian building has been in operation nearly that long. The compound in Hawai'i is more than thirty years old and counting. As of this writing, Victor Baranco's second wife and widow, Dr Cynthia Baranco, lived at the Hawai'i Morehouse and was still active in running the organization until her death in March of 2022.

How does one measure success? How many lives does one man have to change before he gets credit as a visionary? How many books written? How many life-enriching technologies invented? Researchers Bob and Leah Schwartz (both PhDs) studied at Morehouse for a while and then wrote *The One Hour Orgasm*.[3]

Nicole Daedone,[4] who studied at Morehouse in the early 1990s, learned from the highly skilled technicians there a technique of slow, sensual caress called, of all things, "doing." The technique relies on a non-goal-oriented approach to pleasure, meaning the "doer" pledges to not have any goal or agenda, like the intention to bring (or push) the receiving person into a climax, and the receiver also has no goal except to receive sexual pleasure. If a climax happens, it is an overflow experience of all the pleasure the receiver's body is getting. This is harder than it sounds, since so many of us are trained from early on that climax is the goal that defines good sex.

By the way, you may notice we used the term *climax* instead of *orgasm*. This is a somewhat slippery concept, because Morehouse, and Daedone's Orgasmic Meditation (OM) practice, uses the term *orgasm* to mean a sustainable high level of full-body pleasure that does not reach a peak, explode, and then inevitably drop to a lower state of pleasure. The experience of orgasm in these practices can be sustained for a long time, minutes or even hours. (However, OMing sets time limits to each OM experience, possibly because the giver can get tired and lose their focus on the proper way to pleasure the receiver.)

Daedone[5] also has a background in Buddhism, and when she launched her own highly successful movement in the late 1990s it probably seemed natural to call it OM. OMing is a refinement of the process of receiving a "do." In OM, the receiver is always a woman, although the giver may be either a man or a woman. The original Morehouse technique was less formalized and the receiver could be either a woman or a man.

To give context to the Morehouse phenomenon, one of the most successful utopian communities in this country, the Oneida Community, lasted a total of thirty-one years and did not survive the death of its founder. Vic passed away in 2005, and while he is missed, he built a community that could endure. Morehouse is more than fifty years old and still going strong.

Interestingly, Heller ends her seminal work "Basic Sense: The More Philosophy of Victor Baranco and the Institute of Human Abilities" on a pessimistic note. She opines that Vic's attempt to create a "utopian revolution" was a failure. She asserts, in fact, that the whole 1960s utopian movement was a failure, because many of the people that started on the paths of self-enlightenment and alternative living eventually returned to society, got jobs, started families of their own, and became productive members of society.

But was it a failure, really? By what standard? We can hear Vic laughing, reminding you that you are perfect as you are, that every choice you have made to get you here was perfect—and asking, "How much More do you want now?"

6

Church of All Worlds, 1968

In these pages we have met some extraordinary people. They have been explorers and initiators of the poly movement down through the years, often becoming teachers of polyamory in the process. Most of these people have led rather mainstream lives outside of their desire to share nonmonogamous relationships with people they care about. Some of them are lawyers, engineers, accountants, graphic artists, psychologists, transpersonal therapists, actors, nurses, and used car salesmen.

And then there is one man whose integrity and vision have actually helped shape two communities but who cannot be thought of as "mainstream" by any measure.

Oberon Zell—born Timothy Zell in 1942—is a unique, unusual person and one of the true pioneers of the polyamory movement. Over the years he has influenced a lot of what people believe and how they behave in the pursuit of responsible open committed relationships, but he was not primarily known for that in the beginning. In many ways polyamory has simply been a part of his personal way of relating, a side effect of his lifestyle, so to speak. His life-long passion, and the subject of many of the books he has written, is a different kind of community he helped found.

When asked how he developed his philosophies, he talks about how his early childhood reading helped him develop a whole set of different ideas growing up. He explains that his first influences about how to think of relationships between people came from reading Greek myths.

"I noticed that all of the Greek gods and goddesses had multiple lovers," he says, "some mortal, as well as husbands and wives in many cases—and that seemed to be pretty normal and accepted behavior for them." He would later be exposed to stories where people choose to cleave to one lover only and that also seemed like a normal choice for them, but he already knew it was not the only choice for everyone.

If you will remember, in chapter 1 we made the case that the polyamory movement came out of the melding of three very strong social forces of the twentieth century: first, the civil rights movement, which began in earnest in the 1940s; then the intellectual and artistic Beat phenomenon of the 1950s that morphed into the hippie movement of the 1960s; and finally the Human Awareness Movement, which also has its roots in the 1950s and 1960s. Well, we can thank Oberon Zell for at least two out of these three phenomena profoundly affecting the course of the polyamory movement.

In personal conversations with the authors, Oberon reminisced that in 1961 he was one of the "last" of the beatniks and at the same time one of the "first" of the hippies (a word that evolved from *hepster* or someone who was "hep"). He counts himself lucky that he fell into the orbit of, and then was befriended by, an old-style beatnik who was studying at his college. Oberon thinks that influence, along with his propensity to organize and write articles in the underground college paper he founded (one of the first on any college campus anywhere) and later producing the long-running magazine the *Green Egg*, helped him influence the entire course of the student-infused hippie movement during the 1960s.

In the heady year of 1961, Oberon—then known as Tim—was leading the life of a radical college student. The excitement of the civil rights movement and nascent hippie culture infused his campus life, and he was finding his way to being an ethical, spiritual being. He already had a strong background in classical mythology and was becoming familiar with the works of Beat philosophers and Human Potential Movement authors like Aldous Huxley, Jack Kerouac, and Allen Ginsberg. The Human Potential Movement, with its message that you have the power to create who you are and who you will be, was a siren call not to be resisted.

In the fall of that year the book *Stranger in a Strange Land* was published, written by Robert A. Heinlein, one of the premier "hard" science fiction authors of the day.[1] *Stranger* was packaged as science fiction, and on some levels, it was—but it was so much more than that. William H. Patterson Jr. and Andrew Thorton, in *The Martian Named Smith*, devote an entire book to trying to explain the phenomenon that *Stranger* has become, calling it "one of the most widely read and influential social satires of modern times."[2]

Stranger is an exciting adventure story with heroes and villains, it is social satire, it is a tome of parables, it is a modern powerful mythos with appealing characters who come to an understanding of their *humanness* and embrace their sexuality—and it gives a set of consistent and kind rules for the ethical treatment of friends, strangers, loved ones, and lovers.

Upon first reading, Tim fell in love with Heinlein's ideas and adopted these rules as his personal philosophy for how to treat people and conduct relationships—and he has continued to do so for his entire life. He began with his first girlfriend and his college roommate, teaching them the concepts of loving and sharing the novel talked about, without restrictions or jealousy. He introduced the philosophies to his wide circle of friends, and they spent many a night talking about them. These concepts would enrich and influence the rest of his life—and countless other lives—in amazing ways because they worked for him in the real world.

And here we must insert our own opinion, backed up by years of observation: even though the story is fiction, written by an author whose background was as an engineer and military officer with no formal credentials as a philosopher or theologian, the template Heinlein offers for how to lovingly treat people you care about works. And it works amazingly well.

Shortly after reading that book, Tim went out and founded a brand-new religion. That might be overstating the case a little; perhaps we should say he took the concepts of a fictional religion, created by a fictional character, and built a true spiritual movement out of them, with a little help from his friends.

Tim was already not deeply attached to the precepts of Judeo-Christianity. He embarked on a study of European Earth-based religions like Wicca and the modern Druidic tradition, based on the ancient Celtic religious practices of Britain and Ireland, and that led him to a different spiritual understanding of the universe—an understanding in which spirituality and sexuality were combined, not in opposition to each other.

This, in turn, inspired him to take beliefs from the ancient god- and goddess-based fertility religions, combine them with the modern variants coming out of Europe in the 1950s and 1960s, and include the precepts of nonmonogamy in *Stranger*—and this formula set his feet on the path he has followed ever since, leading the way in thought to a new type of spirituality that he perforce had to coin names for. Thus were born the Pagan and Neo-Pagan movements.

On March 4, 1968, the Church of All Worlds (CAW; so named as an homage to Heinlein's fictitious church of the same name in *Stranger*) was incorporated in Missouri and became a legally recognized religion. It has operated continuously since then, a path of spirituality that hundreds of thousands of people have adopted, opening branches throughout the United States and in several countries around the world.

In 1973, Tim Zell met a lady named Diana Moore at a Pagan conference he was presenting at and recognized her to be his soulmate. Diana, for her part, knew it first. Oberon has reminisced in both print and conversations with the authors about the powerful immediate connection they felt, about holding hands throughout the conference, and being unable to bear being apart for even a few moments.

It didn't take long for Diana—who had taken the name Morning Glory as a teenager and was known by that name until the end of her life—to declare her love for him, but then she kind of shyly brought up a possible problem. She wasn't really good at monogamy, she explained, although she would try if he really wanted her to. Well, Oberon wasn't good at monogamy either, although he was a whiz at ethical, honorable multiple relationships. He assured her that her problem with monogamy wasn't really a problem at all.

They were legally married a year later. They chose a handfasting ceremony, a type of pledging similar in many respects to a wedding ceremony that predates our modern version, but without legal standing unless marriage paperwork is filed with a state at the same time. They made it clear to all that they were cleaving to each other but *not* excluding any of their past or future lovers from their lives. They remained continuous companions and coadventurers in life for more than forty years, with a love that kept getting stronger the longer they were together.

In 1984, they added a third, Diane Darling. By this time, the Zells' names had undergone several metamorphoses, and he had taken the name Otter Zell while she continued as Morning Glory Zell. Over time, he would become the now well-known Oberon Zell Ravenheart and she Morning Glory Zell Ravenheart. The Ravenheart name reflects that eventually their marriage came to include several more people and evolved into a "line marriage," patterned after the line marriage described in yet another Heinlein work, *The Moon Is a Harsh Mistress*.

One of the authors of this book, Terry, became aware of Church of All Worlds, the Zells, and their personal path of polyamory shortly after she launched Live the Dream in 1987. She shared some of her reminisces in an article for the LTD newsletter:

> In 1988 I heard about Church of All Worlds. I discovered to my delight and amazement that it was based on the one in Heinlein's *Stranger in a Strange Land*.
>
> The organizers of CAW and I had been walking similar paths separately for 20+ years. CAW was the first neo pagan religion to be legally recognized in the United States. It now has Nests of Water Brothers [people who have created a

special bond to one another and formalized it in a ceremony called "sharing water"—*Ed.*] in many other countries as well. I was very excited as I made my pilgrimage to meet with Otter (now Oberon) and Morning Glory at their home near the Russian River in northern California. During the drive I was listening to a particular filk [science fiction folk music—*Ed.*] song playing on our car system. The words were: "We were traveling north to see some friends we'd never met . . . there were unicorns . . ." It seemed unbelievably appropriate, though I didn't know at the time I'd soon meet a real unicorn. [Among Oberon and MG's many adventures, they spent a decade owning a farm and breeding goats. Eventually they bred a unicorn from a strain of goat. It was a picture straight out of mythology. They spent several years touring the country showing the unicorns off. In fact, the Zell's took out a patent on their unicorn process.—*Ed.*] I found out later the song had been written for the folks I was about to visit. It's been special to me ever since.

Naturally, I became a member of Church of All Worlds (CAW). The magazine they put out, the *Green Egg*, is fascinating and frequently contains lifestyles related material. Though LTD has more emphasis on alternative lifestyles than paganism, appropriate ritual is woven into many of our holiday events. I became a Scion (4th Circle initiate) in CAW on 4-25-98. The initiation was done just weeks after my husband Paul and I shared an adult Bar/Bat Mitzvah ceremony. Did we see a Conflict? No. There are many rooms in the mansion of the Lord and the Lady. . . .

Morning Glory Zell actually coined the term Polyamory in her "Bouquet of Lovers" article [appearing at the end of this chapter—*Ed.*]. Morning Glory and Oberon Zell spent many years in a line marriage (multi-generational group marriage based on Heinlein's *Moon Is a Harsh Mistress*), containing up to ten people at one time.

Polyamory is the philosophy that it is possible to deeply love and be committed to more than one significant other. Some of those who call ourselves polyamorous express this by having a primary partner that we may be legally married to and lovers with whom we may share anything from a romantic evening each month to family activities and nights over several times a week.

Others are actually in group marriages, some of which have been together for decades. Group marriages, intimate networks, co-ops, and communes, are among the many somewhat unorthodox ways we live together. Some of the larger ones fit in the category of Intentional Communities. These may or may not be either sexually open or poly oriented.

THE NEED FOR A NEW DEFINITION

So, how *did* the term *polyamory* come to be?

In a 2004 video interview, Oberon was asked about the origin of the term and began a reminiscence that is quite revealing. The year was 1990. As he recalls it, Morning Glory was in the middle of a favorite and long-running rant about how people in the Pagan community who were in nonmonogamous relationships *just could not follow the rules* about conducting multiple relationships successfully.

She happened to be voicing this complaint to her spouse of sixteen years, Oberon, and to Diane, their cospouse of eight years—both of whom had heard it all before, *many* times. Diane was at the time the editor of the *Green Egg*, the premier magazine of the Pagan and Neo-Pagan community, and Oberon was the publisher. She innocently suggested that since the rules were so important, maybe Morning Glory should write them up for everyone to see, and Diane would publish them in an issue of the *Green Egg*, where they would be read by thousands.

Morning Glory loved the idea and set right to work, pulling her two spouses into the project for inspiration. Sometime during the process, they came to the realization that there was no single term that everyone agreed upon or liked to describe what they do, and they thought that the terms in use were awkward or bulky or just did not capture the essence of multiple relationships as they saw it.

Oberon, with his love of the Greek language, pointed out that the Greek prefix *poly* was already in use to describe other nonmonogamous relationships. There was polygyny, polygamy, so how bout poly- something? The problem was that the Greek suffixes he could think of sounded more like a disease than a desirable life choice.

Morning Glory solved the problem in great fashion. In an interview in 2013 with the cable program *Destination America*, she stated that she really liked the French term *amor*, and also the Latin root *amo, amos, amat*. So she combined the Greek and Latin together to make *polyamory*. An enduring term and the primary identifier of a movement was born.

It is interesting to note that even though the *Green Egg* had been in publication for many years and many of their Pagan and Neo-Pagan friends were in some type of open relationship, the magazine had never had an article before directly addressing the issues of multiple relationships. This turned out to be the article that started a new era in the magazine. It also turned out to be another of the many turning points in Oberon and Morning Glory's lives.

Remember that, in 1990, Oberon and Morning Glory were longtime married partners and had been in an open committed relationship for more than sixteen years. Both had a rich network of friends and lovers that spanned a continent, and both had talked freely many times with friends about the concepts, joys, and tribulations of open relationships. But they did not think of themselves as advocates of an open relationship lifestyle. They were leaders of the Pagan community and were simply living the kind of loving, ethical, and spiritual life that was important to them.

However, shortly after the article came out in the fall of 1990, they came to the notice of the open relationship community in the persons of Ryam Nearing, organizer of Polyfidelitous Educational Productions (PEP) based in Oregon, and Dr. Deborah Anapol, a sociologist and teacher of open relationship workshops and seminars in the Loving More Community near San Francisco, California. (More can be found about Loving More in chapter 9.)

Nearing and Anapol were organizing a polyamory convention called PEP-Con in Berkley, California, over Labor Day weekend 1991 and asked Oberon and Morning Glory to represent CAW at the convention. The Zells were asked not just to attend, but to participate in a big way; they were invited to provide the opening and closing rituals and give workshops as well.

As Oberon recalls, "This was the historic first contact between the poly-sexual community and Pagans. Many of us in CAW, inspired by *Stranger in a Strange Land*, had been polyamorous all along but we'd never made an especially big deal about it. But when Morning Glory coined the terms, we suddenly found ourselves the center of considerable attention. We found our *Bouquet of Lovers*, rapidly expanding. We saw it as a kind of invisible network permeating the growing Pagan community and connecting all these divergent groups through bonds and relationships among their members with those of other groups."[3]

It was an eye-opening experience. The Zells had a wonderful time at the convention, gave amazing opening and closing rituals, and began a new phase in their lives doing outreach to two communities that had interacted all along but had not been on Oberon's horizon.

Oberon would have another experience at PEPCon that underscored just how diverse the search for workable multipartner relationships was. At the convention he came in contact with members of the Kerista Commune, the long-standing San Francisco–based residential multipartner group that had been exploring their concepts of polyfidelity and compersion[4] for more than twenty years. They had a quite different, highly organized approach to multiple relationships.

As Oberon recalls,

We set up a table directly across the hall from the oldest and most famous poly organization around—Kerista, a utopian visionary cult that had been started in New York City in 1956 and moved to San Francisco in 1971. Throughout the conference, people kept coming over to our CAW table after gathering literature from Kerista.

They'd ask, "What are *your* rules?" Somewhat nonplussed, we'd reply, "Rules? Um, be excellent to each other?"

And they'd say, "Well the Keristans have 87 rules and 111 standards."
And all we could say was "Wow, that's a lot of rules. How do they keep track of 'em all?"

After PEPCon, Oberon and Morning Glory found themselves invited to many events, asked to speak on the topics surrounding multiple relationships, interviewed by national news organizations, asked over and over again about the right way to "do" open relationships, to be successfully polyamorous. Oberon never came up with a better answer than the one he used at that first convention—and it's a good answer—just "be excellent to one another."

Life continued to be an adventure for the Zells, and yet, as so often happens in life, people grow and change and sometimes drift apart. The triad of Oberon, Morning Glory, and Diane continued for another three years or so, and yet eventually they came to a place where they decided to part. This is a risky time for many relationships. When a triad breaks up, sometimes it fractures all the way and the three people go their separate ways. Sometimes the original marriage dissolves and a different dyad forms with one of the original partners leaving.

In this case, Oberon and Morning Glory's relationship was strong enough to remain intact, and in fact their marriage would last another twenty years, until Morning Glory's death in 2014. Did they give up on polyamory? No, multiply committed relationships were in their blood and they went on to develop other deeply important relationships that eventually came to include five people living and loving together.

They identified it as a line marriage and took the group name Ravenheart to show that they were one marriage. The Ravenheart marriage lasted for ten years as a residential group living together on a piece of property they called Shady Grove. When they eventually lost the property, it was a huge blow, and while they tried, they couldn't find a home big enough for all of them to live together. Oberon says the group didn't exactly split up, but everyone had to go in other directions when they lost Shady Grove, and everyone began other relationships. The Ravenhearts remained close emotionally, but they didn't live together as a group any longer.

Oberon eventually gave up the publisher's job at *Green Egg* and the magazine went into hiatus. He continued to write more books about spirituality and paganism. In 2021, the *Green Egg* began production again as an online magazine with Oberon as the publisher emeritus. In loving memory of Morning Glory he has graciously allowed us to reproduce in this book the article that started it all. Here, then, are "The Rules," by Morning Glory Zell, complete with the resource list she recommended in the fall 1990 issue of the *Green Egg*. Note: the resource list is provided for historical purposes only. The publications listed are not generally available.

A BOUQUET OF LOVERS
Strategies for Responsible Open Relationships
by Morning Glory Zell (nee Diana Moore)
Originally published in Green Egg *89 (Beltane 1990)*

Let us begin with the a priori assumption that the reader is either currently practicing or firmly committed to the concept of Open Relationships as a conscious and loving lifestyle. If you are not in that category then this article will probably not be of interest to you. If you are full of curiosity about the potentials of Open Relationships, there are resources which deal with such soul-searching issues as jealousy management and theories about why the whole lifestyle is healthy and positive. Some of these resources will be given at the end and herein there will also be found considerable points of interest.

The goal of a responsible Open Relationship is to cultivate ongoing, long-term, complex relationships which are rooted in deep mutual friendships.

What elements enable an Open Relationship to be successful? Having been involved all my adult life in one or the other Open Marriages (the current Primary being [at the time the article was written] 16 years long), I have seen a lot of ideas come and go and experimented with plans and rules to make these relationships work for everyone involved. There is as much variety in what different people require in a relationship as there are people involved in them. However, there are some sure-fire elements that must be present for the system to function at all and there are other elements that are strongly recommended on the basis that they have a very good track record. Let us refer to them collectively as the "Rules of the Road."

RULES OF THE ROAD

The first two are essential. I have never met anyone who has had a serious and healthy Open Marriage that omitted these first two principles. They are: Honesty and Openness about the polyamorous lifestyle. Having multiple sexual relations while lying to your partners or trying to pretend that each one is the "one true love" is a very superficial and selfishly destructive way to live.

There are marriages in which one of the partners will state: "If you ever have an affair, I never want to find out about it." I suppose some folks take that as tacit permission the same way a child will connive when the parent tells them "Don't ever let me catch you doing such-and-so!" Without complete honesty, especially about sexual issues, the relationship is doomed. Some Open Relations have an agreement not to discuss the details of their satellite relations with their Primary partner or vice-versa, but there still must be the fundamental honesty and agreement that other relations do exist and are important to maintain.

The next principle mentioned is equally fundamental: *All partners involved in the Multiple Relations must fully and willingly embrace the basic commitment to a polyamorous lifestyle.* A situation where one partner seeks polygamy and the other one insists upon monogamy or strongly politics for it will not work, for this is too much of a fundamental disagreement to allow the relationship to prosper. Sooner or later someone has got to give in and have it one way or the other. The truth is that people usually do have a strong preference.

HOGAMUS, HIGAMUS, MEN ARE POLYGAMOUS
HIGAMUS, HOGAMUS, WOMEN MONOGAMOUS

The only reason such mixed marriages have actually worked has been because there was an all powerful church/state taboo enforced on options other than monogamy. In a patriarchy, men's deviation from that norm is ignored and women's is punished, often by death. The first recorded gender-specific law, in the ancient code of Urukagina from 2400 BCE, was directed against women who practiced polyandry, specifying that their teeth be bashed in with bricks. Now that the social codes are being challenged, even though the state maintains laws against legal plural marriage, both men and women are more free to explore alternative preferences and relationships are conspicuously in a period of flux.

When I first met and fell in love with my present Primary partner, I roused myself sufficiently from my bedazzled emotional state to say: "I love you, but I hope that we can somehow have an Open Relationship because I am not really suited to monogamy and would be very unhappy in a monogamous relationship." Fortunately, Otter was delighted to hear this as he had been too afraid of losing the new-found bliss to broach the subject first.

Many a relationship has foundered on the rock of Higamus-Hogamus. Nevertheless, the sooner it gets dealt with the better chance for the relationship to survive. It also means a quicker and kinder death to a romance if this basic agreement cannot be reached. Honesty and willing Polyamorous Commitment are the basic building blocks all partners must use to build a lasting Open Relationship.

Once over that hurdle, next comes a set of ground rules for conducting the relationships. Any relationship profits by ground rules, even a one night stand. Nowadays, the state of sexuality being risky, such considerations are more than a politeness; they can be a lifesaver.

Never put energy into any Secondary relationships when there is an active conflict within the Primary. This has to be bedrock or the Primary will eventually fold.

The difficulty with this rule is that if both partners are not equally committed to the openness of the relationship, it can be used as a gun in their disagreements. By deliberately picking a fight just before Primary A goes to see a Secondary sweetie, Primary B can control her spouse and prevent him from ever having successful Secondary relations. This behavior is fraught with dishonesty and secret monogamous agendas; if it is persistently indulged in, it is symptomatic of a fundamental problem with the basic principles. If Partner B plays this game with Partner A's satellite assignations while continuing to pursue his own, B is an out and out hypocrite and needs to be called on his bullshit in no uncertain terms!

Nevertheless, this rule is the safety valve for sanity and preservation of Primary relationships and should be followed with scrupulous integrity. It is a good idea for Primary partners to have an agreed upon set of signals or a formally stated phrase to politely request their Primary to postpone or cancel the secondary assignation so that the energy can be put into the Primary relationship for fence mending or bonding. This ritualized request can be structured so as to avoid loaded terminology and to decrease the negative emotional charge. Frivolous use of this signal is very destructive of it, as is refusal to participate in healing when access to the Primary partner has been obtained.

Territorial jealousy has no place in a polyamorous agreement. However situational jealousy can arise over issues in the relationship when one or more of the partners is feeling neglected. Obviously the best cure for neglect is to focus attention on what has been neglected; the relationship will prosper when all partners are feeling strong and positive about each other. From that strong and healthy center it becomes possible to extend the love to others.

Consult with the Primary partner before becoming sexually involved with a new long term Secondary lover. The Primary partner must approve of the new person and feel good about them and not feel threatened by the new relationship. Nothing can break up a relationship faster than bringing in a new person that is hostile or inconsiderate to the other Primary partner. On the other hand, the most precious people in my life are the lovers that my Primary partner has brought home to become our mutual life-long friends.

The check and balance on this rule is how often it is invoked by the same person. If it is used all the time by one person, this is patently unfair and is symptomatic of a problem or need that must be addressed. This can be tricky and once again, if honesty is not impeccably observed, the rule can be abused. If a man has a hard time relating to other men for instance, he can use his alienation to pick apart every other lover his wife proposes on some ground or other, leaving her with no satellite relationship that is acceptable to him. The cure for this is for the person who has the problem relating to the same sex to seek a therapy group for people who want to overcome this alienation.

Different rules may be used to apply to one night stands or other temporary love affairs. One-night-stands are not necessarily frowned upon and can be a memorable experience, but some Primaries choose to not allow any such brief flings as too risky, while others feel that such happenings add spice and are especially welcome during business trips or other enforced separations. The "ask first" rule may be suspended for the duration of the separation.

All new potential lovers are immediately told of any existing Primary relationship so that they genuinely understand the primacy of that existing relationship. None of this hiding your wedding ring business! Satellite lovers have a right to know where they truly stand and must not have any false illusions or hidden agendas of their own. For instance, in a triadic relationship of two women and one man, there is occasionally a solitary satellite lover who wants to "cut that little filly right out of the herd." If satellite lovers are really seeking a monogamous relationship then they will not be satisfied with the role of a long term Secondary relationship, and it is better that they find this out before any damage is done to either side.

If a Secondary becomes destructive to the Primary partnership, one of the Primary partners can ask the other to terminate the threatening Secondary relationship. It is wise to limit this veto to the initial phase of Secondary relationship formation. After a Secondary relationship has existed over a year and a day, any difficulties with the partner's Secondary must be worked out with everyone's cooperation. If you are not all friends by that time, then you are not conducting your relationships in a very cooperative and loving manner. When all is said and done, what we are creating is extended families based on the simple fact that lovers will come through for you more than friends will.

An additional complication can arise with the variable of alternate sexual preference. A bisexual woman I knew who was partnered to a man had to terminate a relationship with one of her female lovers because the Secondary lover was a lesbian who objected to the Primary relationship for political reasons. Another bisexual couple had a system whereby they were heterosexually monogamous and all their satellite relationships were with members of the same sex. This elegant solution underwent considerable stress and eventual alteration with the advent of AIDS.

STAYING HEALTHY

Venereal diseases have been the thorn in the rose of erotic love for centuries, but recently the thorn has developed some fatal venom. If open relationships are to survive, we must develop an impeccable honesty that will brook no hiding behind false modesty or squeamishness. We must be able to have an unshakeable faith in our Primary partners and a very high level of trust with any Secondary or other satellite relationships. This demands a tight knit community of mutual trust among lovers who are friends. A recent study yielded some sobering statistics: over 80% of the men and women queried said they would lie to a potential sex partner both about whether they were married as well as whether they had herpes or other STDs. All it takes is one such liar and the results can be pathological to all. Nowadays, anyone who feels that total honesty is "just not romantic" is courting disaster and anybody unfortunate enough to trust a person like this can drag a lot of innocent people down with their poor judgment.

In order to cope with this level of risk, a system has been evolving that we call The Condom Commitment. It works like this: you may have sex without condoms only with the other members of your Condom Commitment Cadre. All members of the Cadre must wear condoms with any outside lovers. The Condom Commitment begins with the Primary relationship where trust is absolute. Long-term Secondary lovers can join by mutual consent of both Primaries and any other Secondaries that already belong. If a person slips up and has an unprotected fling then they must go through a lengthy quarantine period, be tested for all STDs, then be accepted back in by complete consensus of the other members of the Cadre. The same drill applies if a condom breaks during intercourse with an outside lover.

Adherence to the Condom Commitment and to the other Rules of the Road may seem harsh and somewhat artificial at first, but they have evolved by way of floods of tears and many broken hearts. Alternative relationships can be filled with playful excitement, but it is not a game and people are not toys. The only way the system works is if everyone gets what they need. The rewards are so rich and wonderful that I personally can't imagine living any other way.

I feel that this whole polyamorous lifestyle is the Avant Garde of the 21st Century. Expanded families will become a pattern with wider acceptance as the monogamous nuclear family system breaks apart under the impact of serial divorces. In many ways, polyamorous extended relationships mimic the old multi-generational families before the Industrial Revolution, but they are better because the ties are voluntary and are, by necessity, rooted in honesty, fairness, friendship, and mutual interests. Eros is, after all, the primary force that binds the universe together; so we must be creative in the ways we use that force to evolve new and appropriate ways to solve our problems and to make each other and ourselves happy.

The magic words are still, after all: Perfect Love and Perfect Trust.

RECOMMENDED READING

A Resource Guide for the Responsible Non-Monogamist, by Deborah Anapol, $15 from Intinet Box 2096, Mill Valley, CA 94942.

The New Faithful: A Polyfidelity Primer, by Ryam Nearing, $8 from PEP, Box 5247, Eugene, OR 97405. See below.

Loving More is a project created by Ryam Nearing who founded Polyfidelitous Educational Productions (PEP). After 10 years of publishing newsletters and holding conferences, Loving More was founded to expand the networking and publishing efforts of PEP. Originally co-managed by Deborah Anapol and Ryam as the Abundant Love Institute, Deborah has moved on and Ryam now co-creates and manages Loving More with her partner Brett Hill. Loving More publishes *Loving More Magazine*—the only magazine dedicated exclusively to topics involving multi-partner relating. They also distribute Ryam's book *Loving More: A Polyfidelity Primer*, host conferences and workshops, and acts as a national clearinghouse and public forum for the polyamorous movement.

Thank you, Morning Glory. You are missed. You are loved. Always. Thou art Goddess.

7

Live the Dream, 1987

Live the Dream is an education and support group for those who, originally inspired by the writings of Robert Heinlein, Robert Rimmer, and Marion Zimmer Bradley, are now ready to LIVE such alternative lifestyles as cooperative living, open relationships and group marriage. Many of our concepts on multiply committed relationships come from Heinlein's *Stranger in a Strange Land* and *Moon is a Harsh Mistress*. Live the Dream also sponsors a Nest of Church of All Worlds, the real life, over fifty years old spiritual movement inspired by *Stranger in a Strange Land*.

Live the Dream is inspired by the philosophy of Family Synergy, founded in 1971.

These phrases, with minor updating, have appeared in the colophon of every Live the Dream (LTD) newsletter since 1987, inviting all who have imagination and desire to drop in, visit, and perhaps find the future they are looking for.

In chapter 4, we introduced you to the premier alternative lifestyle educational group, Family Synergy. Synergy's vision of how to build loving multi-partnerships and strong intentional families would change the lives of many people and have an enormous impact on the ever-evolving polyamory community.

One such person was coauthor Terry Lee Brussel-Rogers. She joined Family Synergy at the age of twenty-two, making her one of the youngest Synergy members on its rolls. She spent twelve years actively learning and teaching many wonderful concepts about loving and sharing, and tirelessly volunteered her time to the organization. At age thirty-four she was still one of the youngest members of Synergy, but the complexion of the group was changing rapidly. The average age of Family Synergy members was now in the mid-forties.

Was this aging of Synergy members bad in itself? No; quality people were still joining and people with vision and experience from other organizations were bringing unique aspects to the group. But young couples getting ready to start families and couples with young children were becoming fewer and fewer, and some people thought that meant Synergy was not fulfilling its mandate.

One of the things Terry tried to do was make sure a large variety of Synergy events were friendly to families with children and to younger members. She recognized that the need to continue to attract younger people to Synergy was becoming acute. People who had the same beliefs as the original members of Synergy, people who wanted to bring their children and create expanded families, were just not joining.

Synergy ran many special interest groups: one was a youth and science fiction– oriented talk group facilitated by Terry. Originally this was a talk group only, meeting to discuss the books they all loved, but over time this special interest group started to see the desirability of having other activities, such as organizing their own potlucks, barbeques, and beach days, and hosting special presenters like Robert Rimmer.

As time went on, it became increasingly clear that this small special interest group was staying closer philosophically to the values of the founders of Family Synergy than the parent group was. Family Synergy was hosting fewer kid-friendly events and shifting to more adult-only activities as the membership aged. This crisis of philosophy included changes in leadership. Synergy founder Chayim had stepped away from his leadership position, and fellow Synergy founder Pat Lafollette had been removed by the Synergy board of directors.

The divide had become so noticeable by 1987 that Terry approached the founders of Synergy separately to discuss the issues she was concerned about. Both Pat and Chayim advised the special interest group to split off and become its own organization.

Terry remembers being torn by this: "I loved Family Synergy; it was a major part of my life. I was dedicating many volunteer hours to keeping it running, and many of my friends were in the group. I respected Chayim and Pat so much and really took their advice to heart. But I just couldn't see separating from Family Synergy."

However, the other members of the special interest group had seen the same things Terry did. She brought the idea to a group meeting and started the discussion. The people attending the meeting were wildly enthusiastic about the idea. Eventually someone called for a vote. Terry abstained, declaring that she would follow the majority opinion. The vote was nearly unanimous. The special interest group had decided to become its own organization.

Now it fell to Terry—a professional hypnotherapist, fourth-generation matchmaker, mother of a fourteen-year-old girl and an eleven-year-old boy—to make the nascent organization fly. But she didn't have to do it alone. Along the way in her life, she had made many friends and allies who would help. Two special people who just happened to be forming into a triad with her stepped forward to help launch the new organization.

Brian Gitt was a personal friend of Synergy founder Pat Lafollete, and while he was not a Synergy member, in 1986 he happened to attend a meeting that Terry was also attending. There was an instant connection. The other cofounder of the group would turn out to be Darrell Smith, whom Terry had met about the same time at a science fiction convention.

Brian, Darrell, and Terry all shared a love of science fiction and fantasy and they all believed passionately in open relationships. They were already building a strong nonresidential triad together, with Brian and Terry as the primary couple. (Their triad would become a semiresidential one when Darrell rented a room in her home, though Brian remained her primary partner.) They were the perfect team to launch the new organization.

Terry took charge of planning programs for the meetings and wrote articles for the new organization's newsletter. Brian stepped into the role of treasurer and newsletter editor. Darrell helped with outreach and assisted Terry with running the meetings.

SO LIVE THE DREAM WAS BORN—NOW WHAT?

From the very beginning, Live the Dream was a cozy meet-in-someone's-living-room kind of organization. Between ten and thirty people would show up for a typical meeting. The topic or presenter would be announced well in advance, and usually the people who showed up were specifically interested in that topic or presenter.

Terry, Brian, and Darrell strove to continue the intimate feeling of the group by fashioning the meetings in several parts. There was always an opening circle or introduction segment, where every person was given the opportunity to stand up, introduce themselves, and talk a little bit about their experience in open relationships and why they were at the meeting. This helped ease the discomfort of sitting in a room with a bunch of strangers you didn't know and also gave everyone the chance to realize they were among friends.

Then the presenter was introduced and would have the floor for about an hour, talking about the topic of the day, sometimes with a slideshow presentation if the presenter was a professional scholar, as would happen with anthropologist Leanna Wolfe. The group would then break for a usually amazing potluck luncheon assembled from items brought by all the attendees.

In the afternoon, the meeting would resume with a planned guided practice of some sort. It might be intimacy exercises like mirroring or guided meditation, or a relationship-building game borrowed from Morehouse Mark Groups, like Hot Seat or Withholds and Overts. These games originally came from the Human Potential Movement and had great power to help a person connect quickly with their emotions and beliefs.

Sometimes a concurrent evening event would be scheduled. Quite often the follow-on event would celebrate either a secular or religious holiday happening in that month. April was always a Passover Seder; Christmas and Hanukah would be combined into a wonderful all-faiths December party. Valentine's Day was always vigorously observed, often with Terry, the fourth-generation matchmaker, giving advice on poly matches. For Neo-Pagans and those who were curious about those traditions, there would always be All Hallows' Eve with appropriate ritual. Then, for the kid in all of us, there was a Halloween party with body painting and scary stories!

During the early years of LTD, the holiday meetings and events were often held in a beautiful, large Craftsman-style home owned by a woman named Anne Friend. Anne was a former chairperson of Family Synergy, a personal friend of Terry, and a frequent adviser to the new group. As a Quaker, Anne was instrumental in advising LTD's steering committee on how to resolve issues by consensus building, obviating the need for voting on most subjects.

Every summer the annual campout to Lake Cachuma (or another local campground) would bring members together for a weekend of relaxation and fun. Even in the months with no themed event, there was always relaxing conversation around the hot tub.

Terry remembers one of the first meetings was a daylong program in how to create a group house: "When I first joined Family Synergy in 1975, a group of Synergy members had designed and were living in a group house, which greatly impressed me. It was called Allott House and it embodied cooperative living, expanded family, and all the ideals I'd come to hold dear. Now, many years later, Allott House was just a memory, but people had continued to talk about how they would like to try group living. So I put together a program about that."

This was a program that actually encouraged people to do a little prep work—homework, if you will—before showing up at the meeting. People were asked to look at their finances and come in knowing what they spent on a monthly basis for food and lodging and what they could afford to contribute to the running of a group house.

"In the morning, the presentation grappled with the ins and outs of group living, how to divide up tasks and responsibilities, how to build commitments between near strangers or even friends and lovers," Terry says. "In the afternoon, people sat down in groups and designed group houses together. This workshop was so popular we made it a regular part of our presentation schedule, hosting many of these programs over the years. In fact, in January of 2020, we were fortunate to have one led by Paul Gibbons, an original participant in the Allot House."

While remaining living-room cozy, LTD was also cutting edge in getting presenters that members wanted to hear. Long before the term *teleconference* became known in the business world, Terry was arranging for presenters to attend by telephone. Presenters who, because of distance, calendar conflicts, or health issues, couldn't be there in person were able to give their programs, sometimes from thousands of miles away. In the later years of his life, novelist Robert Rimmer gave three presentations by telephone. Oberon Zell, editor of the *Green Egg* and founder of the Church of All Worlds, also attended a couple of the meetings this way.

Once videoconferencing became available, LTD made that an option during some of their meetings. Years later, in March 2020 when the COVID-19 pandemic and the world had to go into lockdown, Live the Dream was able to move seamlessly to video-only meetings. LTD returned to in-person meetings in April 2021, but people could still attend remotely, and Terry thinks that will remain an option from now on.

As of this writing, Live the Dream has the distinction of being continuously in existence for more than thirty-five years. Once a month, twelve times a year, for all these years, Live the Dream has had a meeting. And the LTD newsletter has also gone out, rain or shine, to people on the mailing list or handed out at various poly and non-poly events. Originally by mail only and now by physical and email, the newsletter goes out. Each newsletter has a calendar of events, a section of general interest to the membership, and an article, written by Terry or contributed by another member, about some aspect of open relationships.

Terry never knows the kind of significance a particular article will have at the time she writes it. But often someone will show up at a Live the Dream meeting one or two years after reading a particular newsletter to tell her that the newsletter had arrived in the mail (or was handed to them by a friend, or picked up off the table at a science fiction convention, or found online at Southern California Poly Meet Up, or on livethedream.org) and the article was just what they needed to read at that moment because of some issue they were struggling with.

This happens so often that Terry is no longer amazed when she hears it, but it does renew her determination to keep LTD going—and the newsletters going out. A selection of LTD articles published through the years appears in the appendix at the back of this book. We invite you to read them for fun, and perhaps to find something of value in them for your life.

In thirty-plus years, a lot of the history of polyamory has occurred—people's desires and sophistication in open relationships has evolved, and society has changed. The issues and questions people have brought to LTD meetings have changed over time, too.

While remaining true to its core mission, the complexion of Live the Dream is a little different these days. People now join who have grown up hearing about such things as open relationships. They know people with knowledge exist and realize that they don't have to invent everything themselves. They know that others have gone before them and discovered coping strategies for the problems that will always come up when a person is exploring something so new and complex as multiple relationships.

Terry recalls a perennial question in the early days that she would be quite surprised to hear today:

> Couples would often come to their first meeting knowing nothing about poly-amory but usually having talked for quite a while together about whether they want to open up their relationship and add other lovers to their lives. Sometimes only one member of the couple would come first, often the man. One of his first questions would inevitably be, "When I am out on a date with another woman should I take off my wedding ring?" Or even better, "When I am asking a woman out for the first time should I take my wedding ring off?"
>
> This question was almost sure to crop up in the early days, and I found that one very easy to answer. Since the reason they were wearing wedding bands in the first place is they were part of a couple and they were contemplating opening their relationship up to other lovers, it was only fair the new person who might start dating one of them to know their status as married.
>
> And it was critical to the success of a couple staying comfortable with each other, to acknowledge their special relationship in the process of adventuring out into the world of open relationships. This was always a good time to underscore how important open honest communication is between the couple *and* the importance of honesty with whoever might be contemplating dating one of them.
>
> Another common question had to do with bisexuality, or the perception of bisexuality. In the 1970s and 1980s when I was helping run Family Synergy, this was a topic that came up frequently, mostly for men. This was almost never an

issue for women, because women already had societal permission to show affection for each other.

The men would want to know if it was okay to embrace another man or to show any physical affection to another man, because sometimes they would just want to show affection. They were genuinely concerned that the women would think they were bisexual or even heading toward being gay. They would also be concerned that other men would misinterpret their actions as a come-on.

I noticed this question began to disappear sometime in the early 2000s. I did not hear it asked much after about 2004. Society's attitudes about what it meant to be straight or gay or bisexual had moved on. While an individual might still be struggling with defining their own sexual identity, the overwhelming fear of what others might perceive them to be was fading away.

There have been other changes over the years. Even though fewer couples with children walk through the door thinking about opening their relationship to include other lovers for the first time, it still happens, and one of their fears is how it will affect the children. As a mother and grandmother herself, Terry takes special care to spend time with these people, drawing out their concerns and answering their myriad questions.

"One fear that every parent has is, 'Will my relatives, or society, react so badly to my new lifestyle that they will take my children away?'"

Sadly, historically, this is not an unreasonable fear for people pursuing alternative lifestyles. While not every parent had to face disapproving relatives or tensions on the job or crisis with their local Department of Children's Social Services, it has happened. And when it does it is traumatic for parents, children—everyone!

Terry says,

It was the early 1980s. A person who refused to identify themselves made a call to the local Department of Social Services claiming my husband and I were unfit parents because of the open marriage lifestyle we were living. They claimed we were endangering our two children (a boy and a girl). At that time, social services policy was to remove the children first and investigate later! They gave our children to their grandmother, and it took almost a year of fighting with them before we won the right to have unsupervised visits with our own children, and then finally bring them home for good.

This experience caused Terry to join with other parents in 1982 and start an organization called Committee for the Rights of Children and Families (CRCF). She was joined by close family friend and fellow Family Synergy member Art Tarlow, who already had experience fighting for the rights of parents living in alternative lifestyles. Private attorney Alan McMahon, Family Synergy's legal column writer, became the committee's chairperson.

CRCF eventually became a local chapter of the international organization Victims of Child Abuse Laws (VOCAL), which still exists today. It took many years to change minds, and progress seemed glacial. Every year someone they knew had to face what really felt like an inquisition to prove they were good parents. Slowly, things got better.

The attitudes of many children's social services departments around the country is much more enlightened today. They understand that more than half of all households do not fit the 1950s model of a two-parent nuclear family with a stay-at-home wife, a working husband, and 2.3 children. The tireless work of CRCF and VOCAL, of gay rights organizations and other social advocates, have made a great deal of progress to show that you can be a good parent even if you do not look like the ideal of an earlier generation.

That said, if social services does receive a complaint, they must investigate, but they are less likely to act rashly before investigating. In fact, Terry's brother, a deputy district attorney in child services for thirty years, was one of the people instrumental in bringing about that enlightenment. He was known for protecting the interests of the children while keeping families together, if at all possible. Terry calls him her knight in shining armor.

Today, Live the Dream meeting topics might include these perennial favorites: presentations from people in the trenches who are in triads or larger multiple relationships, how to date when poly, how to find poly people to hang out with, and what to do about jealousy in poly relationships. Presenters might introduce other interesting communities that intersect with the poly community, such as the swingers community or the Kink/BDSM community. There are always four to six meetings a year with poly science fiction themes based on books by Robert Heinlein, Marion Zimmer Bradley, Spider Robinson, or Anne McCaffrey.

Terry is a frequent guest presenter at other poly groups, and a favorite question she is asked is, How do I know I am poly?—or even, How do I become poly? She usually gives a presentation that goes something like this:

> Some people become poly after a long monogamous marriage by agreement that both are ready for the zest this may bring to their love lives. This might start with swinging, graduating to polyamory as those involved find that greater intimacy is desired than recreational sex provides.
>
> More frequently, a marriage opens because one partner is interested in one other person but does not want to break up that marriage or is finding sexual fidelity hard to stick to due to a desire for variety. This does *not* mean they do not love their spouse.
>
> There are also cases where a person has gotten into a monogamous marriage or relationship due to intense emotions (aka new relationship energy) and their part-

ner has demanded monogamy. Either the marriage/relationship breaks up when the poly partner discovers they can't live with monogamy, nor feel comfortable lying about it, or they find other options. For instance, they may choose to open the marriage for both of them, or the monogamous partner may decide to stay monogamous themselves, but accepts their partner having other relationships. If that is done willingly with an open heart, it can work out well. If not, the relationship is headed for the rocks. The person who is not having other lovers can consider themselves poly if one defines poly as a willingness to share one's partner and the ability to feel compersion in doing so.[1]

Live the Dream, like Morehouse and HAI, plan on keeping their doors open as long as there are people looking for information about polyamory, looking for ways to enrich their lives, and looking for community. I think they will be with us for a long time.

8

Human Awareness Institute, 1986

Tom Brokaw, news anchor, investigative reporter, and celebrity interviewer, is famous for chronicling the achievements of an entire generation of Americans that he called the Greatest Generation. If somehow he missed Stan Dale, we will try to make up for that, because Stan Dale did some amazing things—and the way he lived influenced an entire generation of people seeking more love and intimacy in their lives.

Terry met Stan and his wife Helen in 1979, when the Dales were invited to give a presentation and workshop at a weekend event of Family Synergy. This was not unusual. Family Synergy members were hungry for any information from people who had insights into how to craft successful open relationships and invited luminaries like Robert Rimmer to give presentations all the time.

Stan was a little different in that he didn't come to Synergy to teach people how to have successful multiple relationships. He and his wife Helen were there to talk about sex and love and caring and intimacy, in whatever kind of relationship(s) you were in, no matter how they were set up, no matter how many (or how few) people were in them.

It would turn out that Stan and Helen had the type of relationship that would stand the test of time, allow them to add a third person to the last twenty years of their marriage, and make for a loving three-person marriage that spanned fifty years in total. But that is in the future of our story; we haven't gotten there yet.

In 1968, Stan Dale was a successful former actor, a well-known radio announcer, and a correspondent for ABC News—and oh, yes, a loving father of six, two with his first wife and four with Helen, his current wife. He was a very busy fellow.

His call-in show on WCFL in Chicago was highly successful, the first of its kind. Stan had originally done a music show from midnight to 5:00 a.m., and during songs he would talk to callers who were lonely and just wanted to talk about their lives. He would listen and give compassionate advice. The calls were so interesting that he went to the station manager and explained what he was doing and pitched it as a talk show covering every topic the listeners wanted to cover, including the topics of sex and intimacy. The station went with it, and the *Stan Dale Show* was born.[1]

Enter his next career. Not quite knowing the path he was about to embark on, later that same year Stan rented a hotel meeting room and advertised a one-day "let's talk about sex and intimacy" event, charging just enough to cover costs. More than 150 people showed up. This blew him away and he decided to do it again and again.

In the early years, the events were called the Helen and Stan Dale Sex Workshops, and he began holding them all over the country, always pricing them to just meet expenses. He would explain in later years that he was making a good living in radio, entertainment, and academia. (Stan had also found the time to earn degrees in psychology and sociology and taught speech at Loyola College for a time.) The workshops were something he did for love. In 1973, the Dales moved to the San Francisco Bay area and continued the workshops, eventually incorporating as the Human Awareness Institute, or HAI.[2]

By 1979, Stan and Helen were on the road almost every weekend giving their seminars and raising their six kids. This was now his full-time job. Stan had not yet written his book *Fantasies Can Set You Free*, and HAI was evolving with every seminar he gave.

Enter our coauthor: In 1979 Terry was a twenty-six-year-old mother of two, balancing a career, marriage, and two lovers at the same time. She had been a member of Family Synergy for a few years. She had never heard of Stan or Helen Dale when they were invited to give a talk at that year's Synergy weekend conference.

Stan's seminar was electric! When he talked about intimacy and community and led the group in intimacy exercises that included face touching and getting in touch with a feeling of reverence for your partner, Terry listened! And she was absolutely riveted by the graciousness of Helen.

Terry says,

> Stan was a very loving man and an amazing presenter. He would be in a whole
> room of people and yet when he talked to you it was as if you were the only
> person in the room. He had a gift for creating connections between himself and

another person and guiding people into making connections with each other that was amazing. Some of it was his trained speaking voice but most of it was the heart of the man himself.

At the end of his first presentation I decided I wanted to know a lot more about Stan, and I spent as much time as I could over the weekend connecting with him. Helen understood how strongly people connected to Stan and she was very loving and accepting of my interest in him. That graciousness caused me to fall in love with her, too.

Over the years, Terry maintained close contact with the Dales. When she found out that Stan gave daylong and weekend-long intimacy workshops through HAI, she began attending them. She says,

> I was a little nervous when I walked into my first Level 1 HAI workshop. I didn't quite know what to expect. Stan had been very clear that HAI was not a 'poly' organization, but a place where people of any background, ethnicity, sexual (or even nonsexual) lifestyle could come and find tools to help them increase the joy and connection in their lives. Even though he himself was in an open marriage he was not going to push that idea on anybody.[3]
> So when I walked in that first morning, I was expecting to be a little uncomfortable and surrounded by strangers . . . and half the crowd were people I recognized from Synergy or other poly groups, and the rest were like-minded strangers. I immediately felt right at home.

In the years after that, when Terry was asked for information about how to build a successful poly relationship, she would always recommend a HAI workshop, often calling Helen to get couples or groups entry into a specific workshop, and she kept track of the Dales' adventures in promoting intimacy and the HAI network around the world. She recalls:

> As my life evolved and my relationships changed, I continued to attend Stan's workshops with the people who were important to me. In 1992, I attended a workshop that had a profound effect on me in a different way, one that caused me to admire Helen with an intensity I'd never known before.
> I have mentioned that Stan and Helen were in a committed open marriage when I met them in 1979. Around that time, I think they met the woman who eventually became their co-wife. Her name was Janet, and she was obviously very loved by both Stan and Helen. He would refer to them as his wives and they all talked openly about their relationship when asked.
> On this particular day, Helen got up and made an announcement to the group that went something like this. She said that she had happily been Mrs. Stan Dale for over thirty years, and after seventeen years in a marriage with them it was time for her co-wife Janet to be able to legally call herself Mrs. Stan Dale. Since the system didn't give her any other options, Helen was legally

divorcing Stan so Janet could have the pleasure of being legally married to him. And nothing else was going to change.

We are not aware if Stan and Helen and Janet ever did change their legal arrangement. However, we do know they remained a happily married triad until Helen's passing in 2003 and then Stan's in 2007. They spent the time together having a happy, joyous life and creating the best HAI organization they could. In 2012, HAI published an article about Stan, inviting reminisces from the people whose lives Stan had touched. Janet Dale wrote:

> To me Stan Dale was the most unique man who ever lived. He lived "out on the skinny branches" of life. Many times in his radio career, as an announcer and as a newscaster, Stan's perseverance in standing up against injustice got him fired, but he never gave up pursuing the truth. That strength had him create HAI, which has touched so many lives. Thank you Stan!
>
> He had the wisdom and generosity to open the space for others to continue the work of HAI after he was gone. The spirit in which this work was created is being continued with our new staff and the spirit has deepened over time. I know Stan is shining down on us with a big smile and saying thank you guys for taking care of his "baby."
>
> Stan touched many lives even when he wasn't leading a HAI workshop. We would be in a restaurant, on an airplane or on a cruise and he would strike up conversations with strangers that would become life-changing dialogs. (It used to drive his kids crazy.) Many women would say to me that they wanted what I had with Stan. I would gently smile, and . . . I don't believe there is another man quite like him.[4]

Under Stan Dale's leadership and under the stewardship of the people Stan drew to the organization, HAI became wildly successful. More than seventy-five thousand people have attended a HAI experience. Seminars and workshops can be found weekly in at least six different countries on three continents. Stan Dale's vision continues.

It seems fitting to end this chapter with several of Stan's most famous quotes:

> "I've always been the opposite of a paranoid. I operate as if everyone is part of a plot to enhance my well-being."
>
> "Comfort zones are plush-lined coffins. When you stay in your plush-lined coffins, you die."
>
> "It all changed when I realized I'm not the only one on the planet who's scared. Everyone else is, too. I started asking people, Are you scared, too? You bet your sweet life I am. Aha, so that's the way it is for you, too. We were all in the same boat. That's probably what is so effective at our

workshops. When I ask, who else feels like this? the whole room of hands goes up. People realize they are not the only one who feels that way."
"Ask for 100 percent of what you want 100 percent of the time."
"The eyes are the landing strip to the heart."
"All human behavior is either an act of love or a cry for love."[5]

Thank you, Stan Dale. A tip of the hat from all whose lives you've touched.

9

Loving More, 1991

If you were someone interested in alternative lifestyles in the 1990s, you were looking everywhere for your information. If the lifestyle you wanted to know more about was some form of multiple relationship option or just figuring out ethical ways of loving more than one person, you were probably getting some of your information from *Loving More* magazine. You might not have known the glossy magazine was just the tip of an iceberg in the efforts of two very dynamic women who had a passion to teach and communicate—and oh yes, throw seminars and conventions—but you were affected by it. These efforts to communicate and reach out would provide the glue that kept many poly people in touch with each other and intensified the feeling of community for them for many years.

While *Loving More* magazine first came out in 1991 as the newsletter of Ryam Nearing's organization Polyfidelitous Educational Productions, it was only the most visible step of an effort that had been going on for at least twenty years. Let us introduce you to Ryam Nearing and Deborah Anapol and you will see what we mean.[1]

Ryam Nearing made her authorial debut in 1984 with the book *The Poly-fidelity Primer*, in which she introduces us to the Kerista Community, a San Francisco–based commune that began in 1971 and would be a powerhouse in the field of nonmonogamy for many years until it disbanded in 1991. Kerista influenced Nearing strongly with their very structured approach to group living. They considered their group a closed marriage, and people had to apply to get in. Every member had to vote yes because you were marrying all of them!

There were no separate pairings allowed inside the marriage, and everyone agreed to keep all sexual intimacy inside the group. They were also known in the nonmonogamy community as having many rules of conduct that all participants had to follow.

In her book, Nearing introduces us to two terms invented by Kerista: *polyfidelity* and *compersion*. She defined polyfidelity "as a relationship among three or more lovers who agreed to have no sexual involvements outside the group."[2] Compersion became an even more important term because it applies to all the persons who are the lover of your lover. It is generally defined in poly circles as feeling happiness, warmth, or joy in another's pleasure, especially your lover's joy with their other lover(s).

When *The Polyfidelity Primer* came out, Nearing was living in Oregon in a triadic group marriage. In autumn of 1984, she and her two husbands started the outreach group Polyfidelitous Educational Productions, and started publishing a newsletter, *PEPtalk for the Polyfidelitous*. In 1989, she released an update to her book titled *The New Faithful: A Polyfidelity Primer*.

In 1991, the newsletter changed its name to *Loving More: A Group Marriage Journal & Network*. The title suggests that her newsletter was narrowly focused on relationships that thought of themselves as, or wanted to evolve into, group marriages. If so, the focus would eventually change, because the greater world was calling and not everybody interested in this lifestyle wanted to build a closed group marriage.

At the same time, Deborah Anapol was also making a difference in the poly community. As both a psychologist and sociologist, she came at polyamory in a very clinical and yet personal way. Over time, she developed a somewhat different focus about what multiple relationships might do for a person's spirituality. She talks about her personal journey in her book *Love without Limits*, published in 1992. Of herself, she writes:

> Sometime in the fall of 1983 I had a startling insight. It gave coherence to my relationship history, including my two failed marriages. It resolved my lifelong sense that my sexual feelings were at once wonderful and out of sync with accepted societal norms. It incorporated my focus on the flaws in family structure which spawn epidemic wife beating and child abuse. It freed me from over five years of scrutinizing my internal and external worlds, looking for what was wrong. Suddenly, nothing was wrong! Everything made sense. And it was so simple: I had really been a polygamous woman all my life, trying to fit myself into a monogamous mold that neither fit me, nor the times I was living in.[3]

Anapol began an outreach to the nascent poly community using her training and insights. In 1984, she started the IntiNet Resource Center and began publishing a newsletter called *Floodtide* to disseminate information about ethical nonmonogamous relationships and to help people network and know about each other. She hosted seminars and became a public speaker, even appearing on television shows, such as *Donahue* in 1984.

Even though she had the resource center up and running and her newsletter was coming out periodically, she says of her first meeting with Ryam Nearing: "Our networking was still so low profile that I didn't learn that Ryam Nearing had founded Polyfidelitous Educational Productions around the same time until we met on the Playboy channel's *Women on Sex* show a year later."[4]

While she and Nearing were running separate organizations and doing outreach in their own individual ways, Anapol was also writing and publishing books: *Resource Guide for the Responsible Non-Monogamist* (1990), *Love without Limits* (1992), *Polyamory: The New Love without Limits* (1997), *The Seven Natural Laws of Love* (2005), and *Polyamory in the 21st Century* (2010).

By 1991, Nearing had been hosting an annual convention called PEPCon for several years, and she was progressively reaching out to more of the community. In fact, 1991 was the first year that Church of All Worlds founder Oberon Zell and his family were invited to attend, and they performed the convention's opening ceremony. It was at this convention that Oberon made the acquaintance of members of the Kerista Community. (His humorous recollection of that interaction can be found in chapter 6.)

Anapol had been organizing and hosting seminars and conferences during this time as well. Being a part of the academic community allowed her to reach out and be accessible to researchers in the fields of psychology and sociology, and since she had a keen interest in spirituality as well, many times these themes came together. In fact, the two future collaborators would decide to go into business together at just such an event.

The year was 1993. Anapol had been invited by Robert T. Francouer to help organize a conference in the Pocono Mountains around the theme of sexuality and spirituality. The conference, called "The Body Sacred," took place in September. As Anapol would recall later, "Bob Francour invited me to attend a '90s reunion of sexual revolutionaries at the Kirkridge Retreat Center." The conference had a clear reason for being: Francouer wanted to bring visionaries together, from science fiction writers to ministers and scholars, from sexologists and sociologists to the people actually in the lifestyle, to "brainstorm ways to further rebuild networks of people interested in sacred sexuality and multiple love and to bring these movements back into public visibility."[5]

At this conference, the attendees were challenged to think nationally instead of locally. What the presenters suggested was a national organization that would pursue the interests of all the sexually open communities. Nearing and Anapol put their heads together and realized they were uniquely suited to do just that. They began collaborating and interweaved Nearing's PEP with Anapol's IntiNet Resource Center. Soon they would be planning conventions together—but something else came first.

They took Nearing's newsletter *Loving More* and turned it into a larger and more substantial glossy magazine, with the goal of quarterly publication and as much reach and relevance as possible. They kept the name but soon added the phrase *New Models for Relationships*, a subtitle that would appear on every issue.

The first issue had articles from such luminaries as sociologists Larry and Joan Constantine, authors of the book *Group Marriage*; and Robert Rimmer, author of *The Harrad Experiment*. Rimmer had been a keynote speaker at the Kirkridge Retreat Center convention that started Nearing and Anapol on this mission. Nearing and Anapol themselves wrote articles in the first issue and would of course be mainstays in the magazine for many years to come. They opened the magazine to contributors from all parts of the poly community, and folks like anthropologist Leanna Wolfe sent in articles. Terry was a frequent contributor to the magazine, even while she was publishing her own monthly newsletter for her organization Live the Dream.

And then there were the yearly conventions. In the view of the authors, the yearly gatherings put on by Nearing and Anapol were crucial to the feeling of community that so many people in poly circles were looking for.

In many ways, the poly community was making it up as they went. For years, people participating in this lifestyle had been inventing new technologies of relating to people and how to build joyful relationships by creating new terminology, new rules, and new ethics. People were hungry for any insights others already had to help them on their journey. The fact that many of the conventions were weekend intensives and took place at lovely nature retreats such as Harbin Hot Springs Retreat in Northern California only solidified the importance of the experience.

Terry attended and presented at as many of these conventions over the years as she could. For her, getting ready to go was always a joyful anticipation. She looked forward to meeting old friends and lovers, meeting new people who might just need a few words of encouragement or knowledge to continue their journey in polyamory, and knowing that this was her tribe, these were the people of her community.

She would often give the orientation at Loving More conventions. This was a chance to acquaint new attendees with the rules of the poly road, such as, "No means no; don't push!" and to advise couples, triads, and so on to be clear on their agreements before venturing out into a more open community than they were used to. Many old-timers also attended the orientations to offer their insights and experiences to all who could benefit from them as well as to connect with the newcomers socially. As a practicing hypnotherapist, Terry also offered her very popular hypnofantasy/hypnomassage workshop. She almost always gave a seminar with her then-husband Paul Gibbons (both of them bi, a bit unusual at the time) on the topic of "Bi-Sexual Polyamorous Couple Forming a Group Marriage."

The convention had a policy of having lunch tables with signs on them encouraging like-minded individuals to connect with each other. Such signs as "BDSM," "Polyfidelity," and "Bisexuality" invited kindred spirits to connect over a relaxed meal. Terry and Paul had the Bisexuality table at lunch for a few years. She recalls noticing that over the many years she had been presenting on the topic, all through the 1990s people were becoming more comfortable with the concept of bisexuality in the poly community. However, one event brought into real focus that the mores of the dominant culture and the poly community had really shifted. Sometime in the late 1990s, Ryam Nearing came to her and Paul to tell them that they couldn't have the Bisexuality lunch table that year. Terry, visibly disappointed, asked why. Because, Ryam explained, everybody attending was already bisexual or too embarrassed to admit it if they weren't. Bisexuality had become an ordinary, everyday fact of life and no longer needed a special table to draw those who identified as bi together.

Most conventions also had a dealers room. Organizations like Kerista and the Church of All Worlds, as well as those in private practices relating to the lifestyle and those selling sexy clothing, often had tables, allowing attendees closer interaction with the people presenting at the convention. Terry usually had a table at which she promoted the organization Live the Dream as well as her hypnotherapy services. She remembers that of all her self-hypnosis CDs on the table, the ones that were most popular were *Male Multiple Orgasm*, *Intimacy without Jealousy for Open Relationships*, and *Sexual Enhancement for Couples*.

Terry recalls what a powerful, visceral experience people have when attending a convention. For most people, polyamory is not an intellectual journey. They want to attend a Loving More convention or a World Polyamory Association Convention, a Family Synergy retreat, or a Lifestyles Convention because they are seeking knowledge and community. These experiences are about people seeking—and creating—new lives and new paths for themselves.

Not everyone could find a way to attend one of these events. To give members of her Live the Dream group a taste of what a convention might be like, Terry kept a journal of one such weekend at a Loving More convention. She wrote it as she experienced it, in a flow state, and published it without editing it in the LTD newsletter. It has since been reprinted multiple times. Here it is in its original published form, circa 1996:

OPENING CIRCLE

Lots of new faces here almost outnumbering the old friends, presenters, and poly icons seen each year. The net with its poly activity actually is drawing some real people who don't think our lifestyle is a new fantasy game.

A lovely woman with an even lovelier voice sings songs which stir the blood and are poly oriented. She sings one about being her whole untamed self rather than "shrinking to meet your expectations" and wanting her love to be his whole self too. . . . "Rough Ride." And so it can be. Her other song at opening is written for the poly family she is part of—Ravenheart. I discover this delightful creature is wife and water sib to Morning Glory and Oberon and therefore part of my own nest. I resolve to grow closer as way opens.

Women's circle Saturday morn and someone's in pain because her lover let her sleep alone while exploring someone new. They needed clearer agreements and she needs to work on jealousy. How many times have I heard this story in 25 years of living this lifestyle? Too many, but each time the pain is real and cutting. Couples attending a poly conference or even a party need (preferably written) agreements to keep someone from getting hurt. Leaving a lover alone who feels abandoned can be as bad if you are poly as if you are not. Consideration and compassion must be combined in an arcane mix with freedom.

A bisexual married couple who have been involved in the polyamorous lifestyle of multiply committed relationships since their teens shares how each of them discovered their bisexuality and how it has affected their experiences in relating to outside lovers together and in bringing special loves into their lives. They are part of an intimate friendship network, some of whom have been in relationship with them for 20+ years.

A workshop on conflict resolution presented by Ivar and Patty was excellent. It seemed to speak directly to some stuff my own partner and I were going through, so I dragged my husband over to it from the video presentation.

SIGNPOSTS ALONG THE POLY WAY

There is a Families Panel which includes Ravenheart and other successful multi adult families. We all field questions with Ryam moderating on what works and what does not, who sleeps with who and when, etc.

Some questions are deep and insightful inviting answers, which require thought and careful wording. Most are asked with an honest curiosity or real need, unlike the conflict seeking of some talk show hosts and morbid leering audiences. The people in this room have either been down this road or are ready to travel it and want reliable signposts along the way. While still a lifestyle of pioneers, we have reached a point where it is not necessary to reinvent the wheel at every turn. Enough people have been doing it long enough to have developed some workable rules which are being shared in this panel and others being presented during the weekend. Articles in *Loving More* magazine, and in Ryam's *Polyfidelity Primer* and Deborah Anapol's *Love without Limits* provide many well worked out reliable guideposts to joy in poly relationships.

The organization Loving More has gone through some changes over the years, of course. At the end of its first year in operation, Anapol amicably sold her half of the business to Nearing, but she remained a staunch supporter and frequent contributor to the magazine until her death in 2015.

In 2001, Nearing passed the baton on to Mary Wolf, a longtime member of her staff who also deeply believed in the organization. Wolf struggled to keep the magazine and conventions on track, a task made much harder by the departure of the very energetic Nearing. One of the conventions Loving More took on about this time was a second parallel summer weekend conference on the East Coast.

Wolf sold Loving More to Robin Trask, another longtime volunteer and convention presenter, in 2004. Robin made many innovations, while keeping the core activities of producing the magazine and putting on conventions, with the help of many volunteers. In 2005, she reorganized Loving More as a not-for-profit corporation registered in Colorado. In 2007, she began hosting Loving Choices hotel seminars, a way to reach a wider public and give more access to therapeutic professionals interested in knowing about this lifestyle. In 2008, Loving More committed to running the annual Poly Living Conference in Philadelphia.

With this wider national focus and having shifted their operations to Colorado, Loving More found it more difficult to continue hosting conventions in Northern California. The annual retreat at Harbin Hot Springs was in danger of falling by the wayside until two other members of the poly community stepped forward.

Sasha and Janet Lessin are Tantra instructors and authors of several books on the practice of Tantra. They own and operate the School of Tantra in Hawai'i. He is a PhD anthropologist and psychologist, and she is a hypnotherapist.[6] They were frequent poly presenters at numerous conferences around the country and had a great love of the Harbin location and Loving More in particular. When the annual retreat at Harbin seemed in doubt, they stepped up and made it happen; from 2012 to 2015, they hosted poly conferences at Harbin under the name World Polyamory Association.

Terry has many fond memories of World Poly conventions as well. One in particular stands out. By 2012, media interest and exposure of the poly lifestyle had progressed to the point that several TV shows were in production showcasing and explaining the lifestyle. This was the year that reality TV show *Polyamory: Married & Dating* debuted on Showtime. The Lessins had invited the cast to attend the convention, and they gratefully accepted. The producer and actors made a presentation at the convention, explaining how the show had come into being, and hundreds of people got to see the premiere episode along with the producer and actors.

As of this writing, Loving More continues to publish *Loving More* magazine electronically on an irregular basis and continues to host at least one convention a year. They also host periodic seminars on topics important to the poly community, with information available on their website.

10

Sex Positive World

Portland/Los Angeles/International, 2009

Next we introduce you to an organization founded in the twenty-first century. Each of the groups and organizations we've met in this book have been forward thinking and yet a product of their times. Each has built on the philosophies and social movements that came before them, and using those insights profoundly changed their present, giving future generations a chance to build on their innovations.

Not all these groups have been focused on multiple relationships per se, but all of them include choosing the sexuality you desire and developing good communication skills to get there. Some of the groups have been the brainchild of one person or couple, while others have been the work of many hands.

Enter Gabriella Cordova and a cast of thousands. Sex Positive World (SPW) does not consider itself an organization so much as a social movement. It champions good consensual sex in whatever form or manner the person chooses and desires. When Gabriella, with the help of twenty friends, founded the first chapter in 2009, they named it Sex Positive Portland. When she formed a chapter in Los Angeles in 2012, that chapter became Sex Positive Los Angeles (SPLA), an autonomous organization. As of this writing, chapters exist in sixteen cities around the world, spanning five nations.

SPW is doing something remarkable for its community in a very structured way, and it all begins with their mission statement and the rationale for everything they do. According to the Sex Positive Los Angeles website,

Sex positivity is a social movement and philosophy which regards all consensual expressions of sexuality as healthy, encourages sexual pleasure and experimentation, places an emphasis on informed consent and advocates sex education and risk-aware sex. Sex-positivity makes no moral distinctions among types of sexual expression, orientation, or identification, regarding these choices as matters of personal preference.[1]

The words *informed consent* might not leap off the page at one, but joyous enthusiastic consent is the basic skill they teach all members. It's how they try to treat *everyone* and how people who join SPW are required to treat each other (and themselves, hopefully).

SPW is organized in a thoroughly modern twenty-first-century way, relying heavily on social media technology to keep members connected and informed. Each organization discussed in this book has had to rely on the technology of its time. Most of the groups we have met in this book started in someone's home, with the organizer handing out their private telephone number and getting mail delivered to their own home.

In the 1970s, a brand-new device called a home answering machine allowed groups to have a phone number that members and other interested people could call at any hour of the day and know that someone would get back to them. As groups grew and got a little more money from memberships and events, a dedicated phone number and a mail drop address might become part of their way of keeping people connected. Eventually, as numbers increased more, a monthly newsletter became an integral part of keeping the sometimes far-flung membership in contact.

SPW may have the power of the internet and the increasing connectedness of Americans in their favor, decreasing the need for physical newsletters, but they have definitely benefitted greatly from the groups and organizations that have gone before them. Some of the activities and attitudes SPW takes for granted today and list in their mission statement were very unusual—even alien—to the sensibilities of 1960s America. Recall that it was only in 1967 the Supreme Court made it clear that a man and a woman of any race had the right to marry in the United States. The fight to secure gay rights and gender equality was not yet fully started at the time and remains ongoing.

When SPW began in 2009, the groundwork of more than forty years of social activism had succeeded in changing the hearts of many Americans. In 2015, the Supreme Court affirmed the right of any person of one sex to marry another person of the same sex. Many types of gender equality are now closer to being a reality. Because of these social changes, SPW may wind up seeming a lot closer to mainstream society than it otherwise might be.

How do they do it? It all begins with an event called Orientation.

Glen attended an Orientation in Los Angeles in the summer of 2014. In his words: "To be allowed to attend an Orientation I had to fill out an application on the SPLA website describing my experiences that might make me a good candidate for this sex positive community. Since I was older than fifty-five at the time, and a straight identifying male, I was also asked if there were any female-identifying SPLA members who were willing to give me a recommendation that the membership committee could consult with. Luckily, I did know a member who was willing to put in a good word for me."

That requirement, while surprising, turns out to have a strong rationale. SPW's mission is to make the environment of every event safe and comfortable for everyone: all colors, all genders, all sexes, and all orientations, especially underserved communities. The SPW website explains:

> Please know that due to the fact that it has always been safer for men to be out as sexual beings, we receive far more applications from single, cisgender, hetero-sexual males than we do from women and all other genders and orientations and relationship statuses combined. So, men, please be aware that although your application may have a higher probability of being declined, please do not let this stop you from applying if you are confident that you have much to CONTRIBUTE TO OUR COMMUNITY.[2]

The policy of trying to achieve a balance of all genders, orientations, and relationship statuses, while admirable, can at times have unintended consequences. Since there are so many more cisgender men applying to SPW than all other categories combined, screening out those who do not seem to be a good fit for the community seems to the organizers like a reasonable way to make sure a more balanced population can attend all the events.

The issue that can arise is that while every person applies as an individual and every membership is an individual membership, some percentage of the applicants are in committed long-term relationships. Some of these relationships will be composed of cisgender women with cisgender men, and occasionally only one person of the couple gets an offer to join. Anecdotally, it seems that most of the time the woman is offered membership. We can remember only one conversation we have had with the community at large where the woman of a couple was turned down and the man given an offer to join. This has been known to cause interesting conversations between the couple. How they resolve it depends in part on personalities and agreements already in place.

WHAT HAPPENS AT AN ORIENTATION?

Glen was invited to attend an Orientation. He remembers, "I was sitting in a room filled with about forty or fifty people. All we knew about each other at this point was that every new person in the room had gone through the same process of filling out an application and an initial screening to see if they have the kind of interests and attitudes that SPLA is looking to promote."

This first stage of screening is intended to help each person at the orientation feel more comfortable and safe, to allow them to just be who they are. Interestingly, it works. Everyone is invited to introduce themselves, and when it becomes their turn, several of the new people mention that they usually have trouble talking in a group setting about things that are important to them but that this group feels safer and they are glad of the structure. That feeling of safety and the reality of that safety will turn out to be a primary goal at every event SPW hosts.

The presenter at Glen's orientation, the very articulate and dynamic Gabriella Cordova, asks people to go around in the circle and introduce themselves. She goes first. Among other things, she explains she is polyamorous in her personal life. Another young woman, aged twenty-two, goes next. She has been helping with the organizing and running of this day's Orientation and lets people know that she thinks SPLA is an amazing organization in many ways and she comes to lots of events, but she is a proudly monogamous woman and has been in an exclusive relationship with her boyfriend for the last four years. Truly, all relationship styles and sexualities are welcome, not just poly people.

After the rest of the circle speaks, Gabriella explains the focus and goals of the group. The group has a very open, all-inclusive but also highly structured approach to touch and sensuality. Activities and sensitivity exercises are used to help people learn to accept more pleasure and joy into their lives. One of the most important exercises at the Orientation will be the ability to practice saying no. Why is being able to say no so important? Because, according to the philosophies of SPW, until you can say no to an invitation or request, it is much harder to say yes—or Hell, yes!—to an activity, especially a sexually charged activity. All in all, this was a very positive experience for Glen.

While Glen had a very positive experience at a meeting, Terry had a more perplexing experience. She says,

> I had a less positive introduction in my attempt to join SPW. I had contacted them by phone initially due to Glen's positive experience with this group. I spoke to one of their LA meeting producers, who assured me I was more than welcome to attend the Orientation and any other event I wished (rated for it by their rules or not) due to my extensive background in alternative lifestyles. We talked about

the possibility of my leading some events for the group—such facilitators being valuable to them as to any such organization.

I went to an Orientation shortly afterward, very excited about connecting with these like-minded people. I brought some of my Live the Dream newsletters, but did not just hand them to all present, being careful not to offend. I looked for organizers to offer my services as a future facilitator and any other assistance I could give to SPW on our similar paths of educating others in joyous sensuality and meaningful relationships.

I must have offended someone, because I was informed following that meeting that I was not welcome at future meetings. That hurt. Later, I heard stories from others who had not been accepted for various reasons. On reflection, I realize that if I was a member of SPLA, I would have had trouble defending the organization's decision to exclude anyone who sincerely believed in a sex positive lifestyle and was committed to following the rules of consensuality. It was probably best that I did not become a member.

Live the Dream and Sex Positive Los Angeles both serve the same community of like-minded folk, but they never did join forces to bring seminars and activities to the community. Both have continued to thrive, regardless.

We have mentioned that SPW uses a very well-thought-out and structured approach to support the philosophy that everyone has the right to feel safe in the community. The last bit of innovation SPW uses in their quest to help everyone feel safe, to be who they identify themselves as, to be able to risk learning more and doing more of the sexy or sensual things that interest them, is the ranking of all events and activities into four levels of increasing sexual adventurousness.

Events are designated level one up to level four, based on the maximum sensual or sexual behavior that is allowed. Each level is clearly explained, and the member can decide what to attend based on what their comfort zone is. An event is rated based on the maximum sensual or sexual behavior permitted, and no person is expected to interact at the maximum unless they choose to.

Additionally, no one may attend a higher-level event until they have attended a number of lower-level events. When a person has attended enough lower-level events, they and the group organizers together decide if the person can level up.

This is how it works: A level one event has no sensual touching at all involved. It could be an SPW-hosted event with a presenter talking about polyamory, for instance, or a field trip to a sexy boutique or comedy club, or just about any activity that is considered ordinary social interaction. Any member may attend a level one event and bring a guest who is not an SPW member. This is important to know, because if the event is not hosted by SPW, the rules of behavior surrounding consent are not monitored or enforced by the club. These are normal social gatherings.

A level two event will have a level of sensual touch allowed that is somewhat greater than a level one or a non-SPW event. Only people that have attended an Orientation, understand and agree to respect physical boundaries, have been accepted as members, and agree to practice the kind of consensually SPW teaches can attend.

All members start off at level two and may attend any level two event. SPW encourages its various chapters to have lots of level two events, and they are very popular—at least the ones that SPLA puts on are. Remember, only members can attend these events, and the people who do are assured that everyone will follow the same rules of negotiation and consensuality.

To attend a level three event and later level four events, a person has to have attended enough of the lower-level events to decide that they are ready be in a more permissive sensual/sexual environment. The organizers also have spent time, possibly much time, around that person and agree they are ready to level up. This system seems to work quite well and may help explain the group's current level of success.

SPW also has a YouTube presence hosted by Gabriella.[3] Their YouTube channel offers a wide range of video presentations about the experience of sex positivity. The various videos introduce a number of health professionals in the fields of sexology and psychology. Gabriella acts as moderator of various panel discussions, covering a host of topics about polyamory and other loving choices. Viewers also meet some of the people who come to SPLA and SPW events and get to witness some of the events as well.

WHAT DOES THE FUTURE HOLD?

As of 2020, SPW has seven thousand members worldwide and is still growing. They are obviously providing something people want. Our understanding is that not everyone who joins a local group like SPLA signs up for SPW, and therefore the total number in this community may be higher. They plan on keeping their doors open as long as there are people looking for information about the myriad choices available, including polyamory, looking for ways to enrich their lives, and looking for community. We think they will be with us for a long time.

11

The Polyamorist Next Door

The Future of Polyamory

We began the first chapter by asking, "What is polyamory and what is it doing to America?" We now ask the question, "Who is polyamorous, and where are they going in America?"

It's not an easy question to answer, because the number of options for relationships and the ways of defining them has exploded in the twenty-first century—and yet at the same time they are our neighbors, and they are us.

We start with a big thank-you to Elisabeth Sheff for the delightful title of our last chapter, from her groundbreaking book *The Polyamorists Next Door* and a quote from an article she wrote for *Psychology Today* in 2014:

> The most reasoned estimate of the number of poly people in the U.S. comes from Kelly Cookson, an independent academic who looked at a lot of research and then compared the percent of bisexuals in poly research to the percent of bisexuals in a national survey to inform his estimate: "It appears that sexually non-monogamous couples in the United States number in the millions. Estimates based on actually trying sexual non-monogamy are around 1.2 to 2.4 million. An estimate based solely on the agreement to allow satellite lovers is around 9.8 million. These millions include poly couples, swinging couples, gay male couples, and other sexually non-monogamous couples."[1]

One question we ask and have tried to answer in this book is: How did we get here? At one time, the conventional wisdom was that polyamory was primarily the interest of college-educated white people of middle-class or higher socioeconomic status. The assumption was that these people were high enough on Maslow's Hierarchy of Needs and had enough economic stability to indulge in whimsical lifestyles. Racial minorities, by and large, weren't interested in structured nonmonogamy because they were overwhelmingly locked into real-world economic struggles and couldn't afford to try anything but monogamy.

Sociologists Larry and Joan Constantine worked very hard to track down and interview a few hundred group marriages in the early 1970s, chronicling them in their book *Group Marriage: A Study of Contemporary Multilateral Marriage,* published in 1973. They used the term *multilateral marriage* in their book and reported being unable to find any black or other minority group marriages anywhere they looked. They interviewed numerous college students as well, and while black women college students expressed a lot of interest in the idea of a multiple-partner marriage, their male counterparts didn't have the same enthusiasm.

The perception of mostly white, college-educated people participating in the various alternative lifestyles may have had a lot of validity in the 1970s and 1980s. By the 1990s and beyond, we started noticing a greater inclusion of all ethnicities and sexual orientations at events and conventions. Although the demographics still leaned heavily toward the college educated and people in the technical or business fields, people from every walk of life were now showing up.

The research of Dr. Rhonda Balzarini and her colleagues at the University of Western Ontario, published in the *Journal of Sex Research* in 2018,[2] support our observation. Their research indicates that these days, the racial and ethnic mix of people identifying in some type of nonmonogamous relationship approaches more closely the mix of general society. The surveys, which several thousand participants filled out, showed that more widely diverse socioeconomic and ethnic groups are participating in some form of nonmonogamy.

Let us return to Kelly Cookson's conclusions, reached in 2014. His research seems to have concentrated on people who identified as couples, and even though that research probably picked up some people involved in triads and larger family groups, it very possibly missed a lot of these people. For instance, whole segments of the nonmonogamy community are not in couples but are in triads or larger groupings. A growing segment of the community now is also identifying as solo poly and would not identify themselves as part of a couple.

The proliferation of polyamory-themed dating sites, websites, podcasts, and social groups on the internet gives one the impression that today there are many more people of all walks of life and all persuasions interested in, and actively pursuing, these lifestyles than ever before. Some estimates have gone as high as fifteen million adults actively choosing some type of ethical nonmonogamy as their lifestyle.

Society continues evolving as well. In 1967, the year our narrative begins, a man and a woman of any racial background had just won the right to marry each other in every part of this country. That was a huge event and arguably set us on the path we find ourselves today. The legal rights and protections of marriage are so profound that people in comparable relationships that are not a legally recognized marriage needed—and wanted—them, too.

This is how the concept of domestic partnership came about. Recall that certain municipalities were looking for a way to let their employees share benefits such as health insurance with the people they loved. Domestic partnership made it possible for a person to designate someone of the opposite sex as their domestic partner, allowing them rights and protections nearly equivalent to the rights of married couples.

The gay community took notice and took heart. It took many years, but eventually one could designate someone of the same sex as a domestic partner. And then, in 2015, the Supreme Court validated these relationships even further and allowed any consenting adult couple to be married, with all the rights and protections that implied.

In 2017, the issue of parental rights led to a triad in San Diego going to court to ask to have all their names on their baby's birth certificate. The judge was sympathetic but struggled over the issue that as a lower court judge, she was not sure she had the power to set such a precedent. She ultimately ruled in their favor and granted all three the status of parent on the birth certificate. Ian Jenkins and his husbands have written a book about their journey: *Three Dads and a Baby: Adventures in Modern Parenting*, which came out in March 2021.[3] As of this writing, they are the happy parents of two children and their adventure continues.

Recently a couple of forward-looking towns have reviewed the needs of people in a domestic partnership again. In July 2020, the city council of Somerville, Massachusetts, voted unanimously to include wording in their domestic partnership program that allowed more than two people to declare themselves a domestic partnership. The nearby city of Cambridge recently made changes allowing the same thing.[4]

The idea that a person can live in the relationship style of one's choosing is no longer an alien concept as more and more Americans realize that everything about their life is a choice, and it is okay to craft the life you want.

We thank you for joining us in this exploration of polyamory in America. We will do our best to update this information and bring out future editions as needed. From both of us to all of you: May you have a joyous, fulfilling, and uniquely self-crafted life!

Appendix

Journeys into Polyamory

These articles are reproduced in the form they were originally published. They have been lightly edited for readability, and some names may have been changed to protect privacy.

ONE WOMAN'S JOURNEY TOWARD POLYAMORY, BY TERRY LEE BRUSSEL-ROGERS

What led Terry to polyamory in the first place? As she explains in this essay, originally published in the Live the Dream *newsletter in March 2012, for her it began in adolescence.*

The year was 1968. My high school offered a brand-new program called sensitivity training. I was used to new programs, all during my school years the school system kept introducing new methods of teaching—new math techniques, innovative science, literature . . . but this was really new. The Social Sciences were exploding with the latest things, fueled by the Human Potential Movement and now it had reached my high school.

My friend Rickey and I attended a weekend event lead by teachers from our high school, Stan Donovan and Bill Gibbons. It was called an "Intensive" and lasted all of Friday night—no rest unless you fell asleep during an exercise. The exercises included touching each other's faces with eyes open and closed, shoulder massages, touching hands in ways that conveyed "hello," "here is how I feel about you," and "goodbye."

How do I remember so much after all these years? It so impressed me at the time that I started leading exercises of a similar nature in my own group of friends. We put together our own sensitivity group that lasted all through high school. I also introduced these exercises to many other groups as I went along through my life, presenting at nudist resorts, at poly conventions, etc. They became some of the basic exercises found at most Live the Dream events.

Both Glen and I were part of a group of close friends in high school, many of whom had read *Stranger in a Strange Land*. The fictional characters in this book shared many adventures together and built functional multi-partner relationships that really looked like they could work in the real world. It fired my imagination, and Glen and I shared water at age sixteen and have remained best friends all our lives. We knew in our hearts we could love more than one important person at a time and have more than one other person in our lives while we were still virgins. We were Poly before the term was coined.

Close loving friendships with several people is a kind of intimate network, similar to an intimate network of friends and lovers which may last for many years. Our sensitivity group experiences encouraged that kind of closeness for me, as did the sharing of water and the formation of a *Stranger*-type Nest of Water Brothers.

Jealousies may be common among such friends, but there was little of it in our group and what there was we worked out through the open communication possible in a sensitivity group. The step from friends to lovers—including more than one lover—was easily taken as teenagers in this situation. Possibly, I would have "grown up" and stopped all that stuff when I got married at age eighteen had not my husband, eight years older than I was, insisted (not that I resisted much) that vows for an open relationship actually be part of our marriage ceremony.

A few years later when I was a young married woman with a year-old child, I developed romantic sexual relationships which were secondary to my legal marriage. Some of those secondary relationships lasted years longer than the marriage—one for thirty years. My second husband was both poly since his teens and bisexual, as I was. The subject of monogamy never even came up. Being bi and monogamous did not strike either of us as sensible.

I have been in triads, one of which lasted five years with all of us sleeping and loving in one bed throughout that time. My choice of polyamory as a lifestyle was initially based on Heinlein's philosophy of multiply committed relationships shown by his characters, presented in *Stranger in a Strange Land*, *Moon Is a Harsh Mistress*, *Time Enough for Love*, and other books.

In 1987, Brian Gitt, Darrell Smith (two of my water brothers then in a non-residential triad with me), and myself formed Live the Dream—many of whose members were in science fiction fandom and whose philosophy was based on writings by Heinlein and others of the SF genre. Robert Rimmer was an honorary member of Live the Dream, and an inspiration to me personally—always willing to talk with me about how to live this lifestyle more joyously until he passed on in August of 2001.

A DIFFERENT KIND OF FAMILY, BY JOE HOFFMAN

Here is another very poignant story of one person's journey into polyamory, written for the Family Synergy newsletter in June 1975. Joe is an individual who gets involved with a couple and joins their marriage, making three.

How did I get into all of this? It's difficult to remember just how it began. In June of 1972, I started on a new job as a messenger clerk in a major public library. One of the first people I met was Mrs. LaFollette. She was a round and friendly librarian who was just a few years older than me. Over the next few months we became close friends, taking lunch and breaks together, and just enjoying each other's company through the day.

Our friendship continued to develop despite pressure from above to conform to the library caste system, which separates the clerks from the "pros" in a desperate effort for status in a bureaucracy where the librarian's position on the ladder is already down too many rungs. All this being the case, my primary objective with Mrs. LaFollette was friendship. I liked her and she liked me. Even though I called her Ann, I was very conscious and accepting of her being married. I never thought that our relationship would ever go beyond personal friendship because of that, although I fantasized a good deal while sorting books in the stacks.

Then a pivotal event took place. I'm an actor by profession. I had an interview (alias cattle call) to go to, and Ann offered to drive me to my car parked light-years away on the street. When we arrived, I asked her to wish me luck and we kissed and embraced. She held on a bit longer than expected. I had to rush off but was anxious to see what would develop the next day. If she hadn't shown me she was open, I probably wouldn't have pursued an affair.

The next day after work we walked to the parking lot structure where her car was parked. She was going around to the driver's side when I asked to come over where I was. She crossed over and I made as if I was going to show her something interesting across the street and put an arm around her. We embraced and kissed. This went on for some time and when it was over, time seemed to speed up. I thought, "Well, smart boy, where do you go now? What happens next? What about her husband?"

All these questions she answered simply after a few more amorous embraces. Where shall we meet? What about your husband? It's OK with him? How does he know? We have an open marriage. He and I both have relationships with people we care about. Well, this was a fine answer, so I decided to follow it through.

Upon hearing of this episode, one of my friends told me that these things don't last. Something had to give—either the affair would end—or hubby would shoot me. I told another friend of our making love in their bedroom, and he started laughing. I told him her husband knows and there was no controlling him. I was told that one night while on the marriage bower, I'd feel cold steel against my ear and my life would flash before me in the last second.

All of my friends who met Ann liked her, and with every meeting would come cunning looks that said they knew what we were doing and that they were accomplices.

"But you don't really like sharing her."

"What's wrong with their marriage?"

"Doesn't she love her husband?"

I didn't like the point of view of each of these because it was misplaced. Clearly Ann and Pat had a very good marriage. The quality of our relationship couldn't have been possible without it. As our love grew so did my image of their marriage, and I began to learn and to believe some of their philosophy. You *could* love more than one person at a time, and not love either one of them less because of it. Jealousy didn't have to be part of a relationship. Their kind of marriage started making sense to me.

My family didn't care for what was going on because Ann was neither single nor Jewish. "Why do you have to bother with her, let her husband take care of her."

Ann kept telling me that Pat wanted to get to know me. I was reluctant to meet him. I was afraid we wouldn't get along. I was worried that if I didn't like him it would affect my relationship with Ann. I wanted to be warm and friendly but still watch him at a distance, see what he was like. It seemed like I was preparing myself to search out all of his defects and then it occurred to me what turn my mind had taken.

When we met, I noticed how slowly he spoke, how long he took to consider what he was going to say. How loud he burped, how his nose honked when he blew it, his ghostly fair complexion. Nothing was good. Everything counted against him. How could she care about him? Oh well, I loved her and she loved him first.

Well, all of these gross illusory perceptions changed. He took time to think things out because he is very mindful of the scope of things. He talked slowly because he measures his words. A good deal goes on both beneath and about the surface with Pat. We got to be good friends, we went to parties together, and the more I saw him with other people the more I grew to love him.

So, we became three close friends. A couple of years earlier Pat had started an organization called Family Synergy, which is essentially a meeting place for people and information on alternative lifestyles. I went with Ann and Pat to a couple of meetings and met a lot of people who had happy families, or very soon to. These people—who had experienced monogamy for years, loved their partners, had good relationships with their children—were here at Synergy looking for or exploring ways to expand their love. This is how Synergy struck me after my first couple of meetings.

Soon after this my friends went to take part in a alternative lifestyle conference at de Bennevile Pines (a Unitarian Church conference center in the mountains). There they met a triple, three people, two women and a man, who in this article shall be referred to as C, C and D. Pat and Ann both seemed to glow with the effects of these three.

So we three drove down to visit them on the following weekend. My first step into internalizing the idea of Ann, Pat, and me together as a threesome came with meeting C, C and D. They were three people whose personalities opened up and drew me close. One sees them and knows how good life can be. I needed this example to think of us together. Now, because I had seen how well it could work. I let myself go forward.

In the following months we lived together, at first I confided my apprehensions about Pat with Ann and she got upset because I wasn't dealing with any of it, I was shoving it on her. So, I started to talk them out with Pat, or understand them as fantasies and wait for reality to happen and deal with that. This became the working mode.

When something came up, whether it be taking out the garbage, cooking the dinner or with whom Ann sleeps (before we got a bed big enough for three), we dealt with it at the moment. The alternative to this is resentment over a series of petty incidents, it seems to me, that just cements itself into a general resentment.

After being together for a few months we facilitated as group leaders at an Elysium (growth center) workshop on multilateral relationships put on by Family Synergy. Questions asked us in the course of the workshop brought us to examine and put into words some of what had been happening to us and with us up to then.

Our friends had, for the most part, been accepting of the relationship. The worst reaction has been tolerance. In terms of family, we have good relationships with our parents, but aren't close-knit with them, so there isn't any pressure from constant interaction. Here again, most are accepting, the worst reaction being toleration. Our suburban neighborhood is relatively anonymous and we have had no problems with our neighbors.

We work well together. When two of us have a problem, the third member stands outside as a neutral translator to make sure that the other two know what is being said. Mostly the arguments are based on misunderstandings. Those that are real arguments are moderated by questions from the third person to clarify issues, or aid in getting down to the real one, and then to facilitate a solution that both will be happy with. So in talking about what we had, it clarified in mind how our relationship worked, and it was good, and it felt good.

After we had been together as a threesome for a little over a year Ann started talking in earnest about wanting to have a baby. At this time I decided that is should be Pat's baby because I had to really analyze where I stood and if I wanted to be a father, and because I thought that it was a natural complement to all the years Pat and Ann had been together.

By the time the baby was due, the idea of fatherhood was really beginning to appeal to me. We all took the Lamaze natural child-birth class together. Our teacher was surprised at first, but was very accepting, and told us that a baby needs all the parents it can get.

The hospital was another story. They had a rule about there being only one labor coach in the labor room. We decided we'd both try to get in anyway. It worked for a few minutes, until a nurse came in and asked which one of us was the father. We told her we both were and she got rather confused and left. A few minutes later we overheard bits and pieces of a hurried conference in the hall outside the room. "What?" "Both the father?" "I've never heard of such a thing!" "They both have Lamaze Cards?" "Yes." "Who's the Lamaze teacher?" "Will someone call her and find out want in h—'s going on?"

A few minutes later the head nurse came in and asked who the husband was. "We both are." She finally put the question to Ann who was in no condition to argue. "Which one is your *legal* husband?" Ann identified Pat, and with that I was assigned to the fathers' waiting room to smoke cigars, watch the Lakers lose, see *Jubal* (one of Glen Ford's more forgettable films) and an Italian spectacle movie.

Between all this poor TV, I'd beg the nurses to let me in, and finally they let Pat and me change places for a few minutes while he went out for a cup of coffee and a cigarette, and I coached Ann through a few contractions. Ann's labor lasted hours. I got Pat some pie and coffee about 2 a.m., Ann's ninth hour in the hospital and twenty-third in labor.

It was four more hours before a nurse came to me in the waiting room and brought me into a hall next to the delivery room to a window through which I could see Ann on the delivery table, and Bryndon on the far side of the room being put through his reflex response paces. I was incandescent.

A little later they brought him out in a baby warmer and I was allowed to look at him for some minutes. He was an ashen pink with blue eyes and red hair like Pat. Now not only were we a triad, we were also three parents.

The nurses were very nice about visiting hours for the couple of days that Ann was in the hospital. We told them the situation and all of the nurses gathered round. They asked me if I loved her, how I feel about the baby, and I told them that we were all "married" (feel married to one another) and that Bryndon is a son to each of us. One nurse said, "I don't know why you're in this thing. Don't you see you're only gonna lose in the end?" I left the other nurses arguing with her. I certainly didn't feel that way.

Ann's mother stayed with us the first week Ann was home. She is a terrific person and she fit in comfortably with our family. Bryndon looks clearly like Pat. So much so, that everyone constantly remarked it.

After a few days Ann's mother became concerned and asked her if I felt bad because of it. Ann answered that she didn't think I did, which was right, but it showed me that Ann's mother was there for far more than seeing her grandson. She really cared about all of us. Needless to say, we were all sad to see her leave when it came time for her to go back home again.

Bryndon is now four months old [when this was written—*Ed.*] and has met all six doting grandparents. We three feel good about each other and our beautiful baby and have high hopes for the future. Though the shape of the future can't be predicted in an open relationship like ours—it's possible that we could become four (or even five) in the same way that we became three—we expect that it will be good.

ALTERNATIVE DATING ETIQUETTE

"Alternative Dating Etiquette" is one of Terry Lee Brussel-Rogers most influential articles. It has appeared in the Live the Dream newsletter in different forms over the years, changing as her own life changed. This version is from the March 2017 newsletter.

If you are a couple meeting another couple, dinner at one of your homes is generally best. Again, as a couple, inviting a single male to your home for dinner is appropriate for a first meeting. If you are a couple meeting a single lady, the best way we've found to handle it is to court her together. Take her out and treat her nicely—let her know that dating a couple doesn't mean giving up the joys of romantic single dating but doubles them instead!

The husband is taking both of the ladies out—he should pick up the check without a fuss. The single lady can reciprocate later with dinner at her place if things work out. If the single is male and you go out together, he and the husband should split the check—you are both taking *her* out. None of this on who pays applies to feminist ladies who wouldn't *think* of allowing a man to buy her dinner—but we've run into amazingly few of those in this movement.

Primary Prospect Dating (or Marrying) Someone in a Committed Long Standing Secondary Relationship

If your partner or prospective partner already is in a relationship with one or more long term secondary partners, you are likely to not only meet these people, but also to form your own relationships with them—anything from casual friendship expressed by a cordial "Have a good evening (or weekend) together," to becoming an ardent lover of that person yourself, if you happen to be bi, and the relationship grows. This dynamic can be even more confusing when your prospective partner's other relationship is as a secondary and has turned down the offer to be primary (or vice versa), but both people have chosen to continue the relationship as it is valuable and satisfying despite that.

There are many in between possibilities. Perhaps your prospective primary's secondary relationship has veto power over his or her primary relationship. This dynamic can happen in BDSM master slave relationships—though the Master or Mistress may be in a primary relationship of their own, perhaps a long married man or woman. Sometimes, meeting and getting the approval of this long term secondary will seem similar to getting the approval of a parent, big brother/sister or best friend of your prospective primary partner.

Perhaps you passed the inspection of your prospective primary partners secondary partner, and now you have created a family by choice. Perhaps they will be joining you for Thanksgiving and Winter Holiday celebrations. Where the secondary person sleeps and whether your partner will sleep with both of you, or that person sleeps alone during such a visit, is one thing you will need to negotiate for the comfort of all concerned. Perhaps you will all sleep and make love in one bed, or perhaps your partner will spend part of the night with one or the other of you.

The secondary partner may be long distance, taking your partner away for a weekend a few times a year, or you may be sharing the bed with them twice a week if that secondary is local and available for such things—some call this a semi residential triad such as the one which originally founded Live the Dream.

It is wise to find out what the current situation is before getting into such a relationship. You may be able to negotiate changes which would make you more comfortable either to start with or ongoing. While it is not a given that you will take the time commitments in that relationship as is, you will most likely be expected to accept the relationship itself, which may have been going on for decades.

The honest and ethical thing for you as someone forming a primary relationship with a person in such a relationship is to be clear on what you can handle and what you can't, so your prospective primary partner can make an informed choice about what he or she is committing to. Changing the rules after the wedding, handfasting or decision to live together is something which would have to be done by mutual consent—perhaps including the consent and input of the secondary partner. Arbitrary vetoes or changes at this point have been known to end in a breakup of the new primary relationship, so think carefully about it—and be fair to yourself as well your partner and the person who may have seen him or her through 3 marriages, perhaps helping to raise kids involved.

Three in the Car

If you all go out together as three, the wife and single lady should alternate sitting in the front seat if your car has bucket seats. In the case of a couple dating a single man, the gentleman whose car is being driven will usually drive with the lady beside him. Three in front is much better if you have a vehicle which can do it—rare as of 2015.

Three at a Restaurant

If you are going to a restaurant, plan things so that round booth seating (preferable) or individual chairs around a table that will help the couple not arrange to be sitting on one side and the single on the other. Whether that single is male or female, avoid anything with a two against one feel to it. Call ahead to check exactly what kind of seating the place has if you have not been there before.

Couples Together and Apart

Be sure you not only do the obvious of sitting in cars or restaurants with the opposite sex member of the other couple, but spend time with the same sex one, too. This goes for separate meetings as well. The gentlemen can go to a computer fair together while the ladies go for a drive or whatever. Remember, you are *all* in a relationship together, trying to make this thing work out.

During 50 years of living this lifestyle, I have found that the relationship between same sex members of a triad, quad or bigger group is *at least* as important as that between opposite sex members, especially if the same sex members are hetero. I will never forget the man whose "share" at a Loving More conference was that, "This woman is the lady I love, ardently desire, and want to spend the rest of my life with. This is the man I want to repair roofs and remodel kitchens with for the rest of my life. I love them both equally in different ways."

I hear also in my mind Marcus saying to Paul and me early in our relationship, when we were just beginning to relate as a triad, "I've got to tell you, I love you both!" in joy and surprise. His first triad was with his best friend from high school—he expected to love both his bride and the man he asked to join them in their marriage. Paul (in 2000, several months before our braiding ceremony in June 2001) was a much newer friend, in time to become even closer to him than that high school buddy.

Separate Dating—Couple with a Single

Depending on the couple's comfort level with it, after getting to know them both on two or three joint meetings, you as a single male could offer to take the lady alone out for lunch, dinner or even a play. This works particularly well if her husband gets to go to some meeting or activity he is really interested in but she is not. This way you get to entertain her. You, as the male member of a couple, can also ask the single lady out, assuming this is ok with your wife—best to have your wife assure her that it is, especially if your previous meetings have been as three.

Quadrad Complication

Here is a situation that might occur when two couples, composed in this case of a husband and wife, have built a household together: You and your husband have a date for an intimate evening with a couple that are not the other couple in your quadrad, but whom you know well and are already in a relationship with. The other man in your quadrad comes in after a sweaty job for a shower. He takes the shower, comes out and gets eye contact with your husband's date (with whom he has had ample previous contact) and joins them in bed.

They have a lovely time, but when wife #2 gets back from her date she is angry at not to have been consulted about her exclusion from this date with the visiting couple. This is discovered when that couple goes home and husband #2 attempts to come to bed. He finds his clothes, etc., tossed outside the door of the bedroom of wife #2, with a Do Not Disturb sign on her door. He sleeps with his other wife and husband while she sleeps alone.

Whether wife #2 (who has joined the triad after they had been together five years) has reason to be disturbed depends on several factors: How well does she know the visiting couple? Would they have been comfortable with her being added into the mix? Was she told previously that this would be a private date between the original couple and their guests? Would it have been reasonable for Husband #2 to have disturbed her during her date to ask if it was ok for him to join the other couples in bed? Is she comfortable being by herself upon occasion—or not?

Some things are a bit spontaneous at the time and the only way to avoid upset is to discuss a lot of hypotheticals in advance, realizing that you can't cover them all. Write down what you will do about the hypotheticals. When one comes up which has not been previously discussed, give your partners the benefit of the doubt and decide among you how this could best be handled in the future to create a win-win for all involved rather than getting upset that the situation wasn't handled properly this time.

The above situation could have occurred in a triad without the fourth partner. In our case, husband #2 was frequently not included in our dates with other couples or singles for a number of reasons, ranging from their comfort level with his extra weight to whether the dynamics of that particular situation made it best for him to be included at that time. He was not interested in being included when the single was male, for example.

In other cases where he might have wanted to be included, he accepted that it just wasn't going to happen with this person or couple or on this occasion. We worked all this out long before we became a quad. Some of our standing rules probably needed to be renegotiated or at least clarified with a fourth person in the mix.

Much of what affects the above scenario comes down to whether separate dating is ok at all, or if all must be included every time. I am not comfortable with an all or nothing rule. It is too limiting for me, particularly when I had relationships predating any of those I had with my quad. Others accept all or nothing as the price of having committed relationships or a marriage. Some even accept monogamy as the price of such a relationship.

HOW DOES A POLY PERSON
FIND TIME ENOUGH FOR LOVE,
BY TERRY LEE BRUSSEL-ROGERS

This article, about poly time management, was originally published in the Live the Dream newsletter in October 2009.

There are 168 hours in your week. Are you using them effectively in your personal as well as your business life? We are about to find out!

As a hypnotherapist, I help my clients manage their time to get the most out of it for reaching both financial and personal goals. As a matchmaker, I frequently have had to advise my clients about how to make time in their lives for a special someone or even just how to find the time to meet the possible special someone's I am matching them with.

Time management is needed for all of this. It might seem cold and calculating, but if you don't do it, you will find something, or *someone*, gets the short end of the stick. Your own rules (agreed upon with your primary partner if any) about how to use your time will insure quality time with all those who are dear in your life.

Make a list of your most important relationships. This means with your kids, your mother, and your best friend as well as your mate and your lover(s). This will not include all your friends and cousins. Those people will be lumped together under "Socializing" and will be fit into the time reserved for that. Make note of which of these most important people can be visited together, which you prefer to see separately, and which get both shared and alone time.

Now to give you an idea—Relationships in my life:

1. A Husband.
2. A Daughter who has a daughter and a son.
3. A Son who has two daughters.
4. Two housemates.
5. A non-residential lover.
6. Best friend/water brother Glen. Water brothers may or may not be my lovers at any moment. Irrelevant, as close friendships take time to maintain, too.

7. When I was looking for a possible primary partner, I spent about 7 hours a week, both reaching out on websites and dating.

8. Time spent with my water brothers and relatives, 6 hours per week. Some of my relationship time is counted elsewhere as eating time, time spent on Live the Dream, etc. Glen gets 2 and a half hours twice a month of alone time and one day a month doing something like going to Ventura Harbor or Disneyland with his 7 yr. old son. Rick is a non-residential lover who spends half his time out of the country and most of the rest of it out of state. We spend perhaps four weekends a year together. These are full days and evenings—32 hours a year divided by 52 for alone time and 32 already counted as time with water brothers. Sleep time is also counted elsewhere. And so forth.

You'll notice that I spend regularly scheduled time with the people in my life. Some of my relationships have been deep and delicious for over twenty years. I also run two businesses and find time to play with my grandchildren. I regularly add to and update an extensive manual for professional hypnotherapists as well as creating new books and CDs for laymen interested in that topic.

I couldn't possibly do all of this without a system. The people who love me know that by assigning them a set time, I'm honoring what we mean to each other. Naturally, it has to be flexible enough to accommodate changes when they arise. More on that below.

Now I'm going to give you times to note that are the number of hours or minutes most people take for these things. Some of them will not be correct for you. If they aren't, use the times that reflect your real life. You are probably going to have to make a time log after this to accurately record how you are actually spending your time, but we're going to start with some guesses about what's happening.

Eating: Most people take 1½ hrs. a day to eat—10.5 hrs. a week. If that is right for you, note it. Do you spend more time on eating on weekends, but less during the week? It may average out.

Sleeping: Do you sleep 6-7-8 hours a night? Six hours during the week with an extra couple of hours for weekends nights comes to 46 hours a week. Shopping for groceries averages 2 hours a week for most people. Exercise should take at least 3.5 hours a week—reserve that time and use it—it can make your LOVE exercises better for both/all of you. Personal Toiletries such as showering, shaving, dressing, and sitting on the throne amount to 10.5 hours a week, usually. There is a lot more and yes you do have to get this detailed to be accurate. Everything from phone time with Mom in New York to Sabat at the

Full Moon should be counted. Education and fornication all take time. Don't forget driving or flying time in long distance relationships.

Add up all the times you have listed. If the total is only 140—you've missed something . . . or someone. If it is 210, don't freak because you've probably counted things twice. Hey, didn't you notice your husband in the bed when your girlfriend was cuddling you? Gotta pay attention. You already counted this as shared socializing time with him.

Filling Out Time Management Schedule

Fill in first the things which you do regularly and do not have the option of changing in most cases. These will include class schedules for students, work hours for those not self-employed, taking kids to school for parents, etc. Then the more flexible items should be filled in with a vertical line down the middle for first and second choice of how to use that time.

Examples: One option is alone time with your lover. If your lover is busy (couldn't he *share* her with you?), the other option may be spending extra quality time with your husband (or even your vibrator and a sexy book if hubby is elsewhere). Be sure to list all options in any case requiring the participation of other people, or anything you can't directly control, such as the weather.

Make sure that steps to accomplishing goals and pleasurable time to do what you enjoy most are both included on this schedule. Post the filled out schedule at home with an (edited) one at the office. Keep a copy in the glove compartment of your car. At any given time, it should be possible to check this schedule to find out what you are committed to doing right now.

This avoids such time wasting as "seeing what's on tv" when the weather does not permit a scheduled walk, or your business coach cancels an appointment. Both options will always be in the same general category as the other option. Choose what you do that is *most* pleasurable (as well as practically doable) with the time scheduled for pleasure. Take care of yourself and *enjoy*. You deserve it!

COMING OUT POLY,
BY TERRY LEE BRUSSEL-ROGERS

Originally published in the Live the Dream newsletter in August 2014

In my many years of doing alternative lifestyles counseling and doing support and education groups for this community, I have encountered many different situations and questions about whether and how one should come out poly. This is a list of some of the most frequently asked questions and the best answers I've devised for them. I'll be happy to answer any questions *you* care to submit in a future article.

Q: Should we tell our teenage children about our lifestyle?

A: Unless you are either very discrete and/or hypocritical in your discussions of sexual love with these "children," they already suspect you have an unorthodox lifestyle. Teenagers are far more aware and intelligent about such things than many parents realize. If they do suspect, but have not been told, they feel distrusted. If they don't suspect but find out in any number of ways on their own, they are likely to be shocked, hurt or angry.

The safest, most caring thing to do is tell them yourselves, handle their questions (as well as any possible emotional upset) as fully, honestly, and compassionately as you can. Be sure they understand that this is something you believe in rather than something you are ashamed of. Let them know, too, that their own choice of lifestyle is up to them and that you will support them in the choices they make.

The question of whether to tell younger children comes up too. I raised my children in a marriage which was open from the beginning. Our four year old daughter discovered this by finding my husband in bed with a female friend of the family one morning. She came into the other bedroom to find me in bed with this lady's husband. She said "Mommy, Daddy is in bed with Grace. Oh! You're in bed with Roy!" There was nothing going on but cuddling—both of us hugged her and said this was how we chose to express our love for each other.

We told her all of us loved her, too, in a different way. She seemed satisfied with that. It probably would have been more difficult if these were not two people who we had over many times and who had taken her on picnics, to the zoo, etc. If that had not been the case, we would not have been in bed with them in all probability—certainly not where a child could walk in and be upset by it.

It was always our policy not to do anything which would likely be upsetting to our children and to answer their questions honestly when they came up. The bottom line is not to be doing anything you yourself feel less than proud of. Children will certainly sense it if you are always hiding something from them.

Q: From a divorced mother concerned about her ex-husband's reaction if he finds out she has become poly: Should I tell my teenaged children about my lifestyle?

A: See above, but you may need to add the request not to share this with Dad, who may be needlessly upset by it. You take your chances on this one—your teenager may discuss it with the other parent, and if it sufficiently upsets him/her or if the family situation is such that he benefits from playing one parent against the other. Custody issues are touchier with younger children but can still be a factor in cases like this. Ideally, you would share it first with your ex, discuss if/how to reveal your lifestyle to the teenager(s), and show a united front on this issue. That only works if you have a good relationship with your ex, and habitually discuss matters effecting the children's welfare.

    If you choose not to chance coming out to your children in a divorce situation, be *very* discrete in your behavior as being found out by accident can be far more explosive here.

Q: My parents don't know I'm in a triad. They've met their grandson, but think he is the son of my co-husband—our lady's legal mate. Should I risk their upset over a lifestyle in conflict with their strict Catholic beliefs or deprive them of the joy of a long hoped for grandchild by their only son?

A: I advised this man to tell his parents the truth as I believed the delights of grandparenthood would outweigh their disapproval of his chosen lifestyle. Things were stormy between them for a while—more because his parents felt they should have been told from the start rather than with the child reaching age two than from their disagreement on lifestyles issues, though that was certainly in there.

    The man in the above example was a friend. He said at the time I gave it that my glib advice was fine for me because I would not have to live with the results. I decided to take the challenge and come out Bi with my mother (about the only kind of coming out I had not already done with my family). She was *really* upset and did not have the prospect of something as wonderful as a new grandchild to console her. As an old woman in a rest home, did she really need to know this? Probably not.

    Need to know vs. upset factor is, I think, the key here. Your Christian fundamentalist aunt and uncle who live across the country and see you once a year at the family reunion probably don't need to know about your lifestyle. If they are coming to spend a week staying in the same house with you and your two wives—better tell them. Asking one of your wives to act like she's "just a roommate" for a week is another option, but not one I would advise. In my home, I ask stay over visitors to be decently tolerant of my lifestyle or see me elsewhere.

Q: Should I discuss my lifestyle at work?

A: Generally not, if any risk to employment or promotability is present. It is no one's business but your own and that of those close to you. If it becomes appropriate to mention it due to some attraction you may have to a co-worker who would treat you as verboten if you were married, you are taking the usual risks in getting involved with someone at work who may not work out long term romantically, plus the added risk that this person will "out" you against your wishes. Take care!

If you are the boss, revealing your lifestyle involves the risk, if you are male, of causing female employees to take innocent actions on your part as sexual harassment. As a woman, this has not been a problem for me, nor do I believe most women need to worry about it as a boss. At worst, it may invite unwanted passes which you can diplomatically rebuff. It can't get you fired, but whether it is worth the hassle or not is questionable. If you are actually in an established triad, coming out may be worthwhile so that both your significant others can be present for company picnics, etc.

I tell my employees about the lifestyle since I deal with poly issues in my business both as a hypnotherapist and a matchmaker. Also, I have always been very public about my lifestyle as a presenter on the topic.

REPORT ON THE HEINLEIN CENTENNIAL, BY TERRY BRUSSEL-GIBBONS

Robert A. Heinlein is mentioned many times in this book as an inspiration for some people choosing a poly lifestyle. Here is a bit more info on this well-regarded author. This article originally appeared in the August 2007 Live the Dream newsletter.

On Heinlein Centennial Celebrated July 5–July 8, 2007, at Kansas City's Hyatt Regency Hotel. This was the 100 year anniversary of the birth of Robert A. Heinlein, Grand Master of Science Fiction.

I had some difficulty in getting the subject of polyamory on the schedule for this convention. Some of the organizers were of the opinion, which had also plagued me at science fiction conventions on several occasions, that those of us who were inspired in our choice of lifestyle by some of Heinlein's writings were "Heinlein's Bastard Children." They based this on an opinion that the books which had so affected my life and those of many like me were meant by the author to be "only fiction" rather than something he meant to be taken seriously and used in creating a way of relating to others in one's life.

The answer to that (and what finally allowed me to get poly programming into the Heinlein Centennial Celebration) is this: Heinlein wrote his first novel *For Us the Living* in 1938 (discovered in someone's attic and finally published 2004) with open marriage and freedom from jealousy as one of its major themes. *The Moon Is a Harsh Mistress* and (of course) *Stranger in a Strange Land* have these themes as well. So did all of his Lazarus Long novels, from *Time Enough for Love* through his final novel, *To Sail Beyond the Sunset*. Group marriages are shown in detail, from who sleeps with whom and how they relate to each other, to how property is handled, and children are raised.

William H. Patterson Jr., cofounder of the Heinlein Society and Robert A. Heinlein's official biographer, thoroughly researched the issue and showed that Heinlein actually lived in an open, committed relationship during his marriage to Leslyn MacDonald, which lasted fifteen years. He has evidence that Robert Heinlein believed in what we now call polyamory throughout his life, whether actively practicing it or not. The idea that he was "just writing stories" about this lifestyle was truly put to rest. He believed in what he was writing, and we salute him as teacher and inspiration for so many of us who believe you can love and be deeply committed to more than one significant other.

Mr. Patterson is the only author ever to be given full access to the Heinlein family's archives. The biographer saw stories from Heinlein's early life that were very similar to the early lives of Maureen and Lazarus in *To Sail Beyond the Sunset* and *Time Enough for Love*. Heinlein's early experiences in Kansas City's political machine influenced the political writings in his juveniles as well as the more sophisticated political commentary in *Stranger in a Strange Land*. Most importantly for those of us in the poly lifestyle, we learn that Heinlein, who was in an open marriage before his marriage to his second wife Virginia, believed it was possible to deeply love more than one significant other. In this biography, as in Heinlein's first novel *For Us the Living*, we find the seeds for nearly all of the Heinlein writings we have loved and learned from. If you have questions about Heinlein's life and beliefs, do read *Robert A. Heinlein in Dialogue with His Century*, volumes 1 and 2.

The Heinlein Society, which celebrated its twentieth anniversary in August of 2020, provides Heinlein's books, educational CDs and downloads to Middle School, High School, and College classes and libraries, publishes the *Heinlein Journal*, and has sent 30,000 of Heinlein's books to active military personnel and veterans around the world.

Terry and Paul Brussel-Gibbons moderated three Families-themed panels with an emphasis on polyamory at this convention. They were:

Chosen Family: How Heinlein has affected family structure in Real Life families.

Families in Heinlein: From the Rolling Stones to the Long clan to line marriages: families were heavily featured in Heinlein.

I Now Pronounce You: A look at the different models for relationships (such as line marriages) and the ceremonies with which those commitments were made in the stories and in reality.

We had great turnouts for all of these panels—40 to 50 for each of them. It was a mix of people, from those who were just curious after reading Heinlein's books to the people who had been living in a 5 person group marriage since 1985 and were now promoting a weekly pod cast on poly living. That Quint had actually gone to the trouble of doing the legal work to have their arrangements made into a contract which recognized their joint ownership of the home in which they lived and gave them spousal rights in cases of illness or death. The line marriage ceremony in *The Moon Is a Harsh Mistress* and the group marriage in *Time Enough for Love* were discussed, as were the real life ceremonies some of us had used for our own marriages. Heinlein's group marriages are about the adults promising to take care of children, protect the women while they have those children, preserve assets, and have fun together while accomplishing all this. Ritual and public commitment are the keys to success, both in Heinlein's books and according to people who have done group marriage successfully.

Glossary

People have been grappling with a way to describe the changing landscape of human relationships in this country for a very long time. The Mormons coined the term *plural marriage* in the 1820s to describe their version of church-sanctioned marriage involving more than two persons. In the 1850s, the Oneida Community invented the term *complex marriage* to help them explain to themselves and others what they were doing.

In the hopes that it will help the reader, we have compiled a list of terms Americans have been using to help define and describe the relationships we have been inventing for the last couple hundred years.

RELATIONSHIPS THE PARTICIPANTS SOMETIMES CALLED MARRIAGE

companionate marriage: This term was coined in the 1920s by sociologists to describe a style of relationship often built around a legal marriage, where the partners have mutual consent and equality. Its purpose is founded on companionship rather than focusing on traditional marriage values (e.g., raising children). One partner might not be expected to provide all or most of the financial support. In this envisioned style of marriage, the couple might make the radical choice to use birth control to choose the size of their family, and divorce would happen by mutual consent.

complex marriage: As coined by the Oneida Community, this is a form of group marriage where every man in the group considered himself married to every woman, and every woman in the group considered herself married to every man. *See* polyfidelity.

closed/open marriage: A traditional closed marriage (or closed relationship) is one where the couple chooses to have no other sexual (and/or emotional, and/or romantic) partners. In an open marriage (or open relationship), the partners have agreed on some rules that allow one or both partners to have other sexual (or emotional or romantic) partners.

group marriage: In this arrangement, three or more adults have made long-term emotional and sometimes financial commitments to one another, generally sharing living quarters. It has also been called *conjoint marriage*.

plural marriage: This term describes one man married to two or more women within the Mormon religion. This form of marriage was at one time sanctioned by the Church of Jesus Christ of Latter-day Saints.

trial marriage: A term referring to a limited period of cohabitation between two people. At the end of the trial period, the couple either marry or dissolve the relationship. Although never a legal form of marriage in the United States, it has been talked about since the 1920s.

TERMS TO DESCRIBE OTHER RELATIONSHIPS

primary relationship: In psychology, this is a person's closest relationship. This term was adopted and popularized by Family Synergy to mean the loving relationship closest or most central in a person's life. This is the person they might spend the largest part of their time with, share finances with, share living space with, and/or raise children with.

secondary relationship: This is a loving relationship further out from the center of a person's life. The emotional bond may be very strong, but a secondary relationship may not involve seeing the person as often as a primary and is less likely to involve interweaving finances, property, or childrearing. A person may have multiple secondary relationships without being in a primary relationship.

tertiary relationship: This is a relationship less involved than either primary or secondary. The emotional relationship may be very strong with the tertiary partner, but sharing resources may be minimal, and time spent will be much less than with a primary or secondary partner.

dyad: This is a two-person relationship.

triad: This is a three-person relationship.

V-style triad: In a three-person relationship, the V, sometimes called the hinge partner, is the person that the other two partners usually have the strongest relationship with. Being in a triad does not necessarily imply that all partners have sex with each other. For instance, in the case of a triad where two people of the same sex are not bisexual, they may only have sex with the partner of the opposite sex, but they may still have very strong emotional bonds with the partner of the same sex.

quad: This is a four-person relationship. Quads may be composed of two couples, may have started as a triad that has added a fourth, or may be composed of four separate individuals who have come together to make the relationship. Generally speaking, if there are more than four people in the relationship, they stop counting the number of people and just consider themselves a group relationship.

mono/poly relationship: This term is usually used by couples to describe that the couple has an agreement that one of them chooses to be monogamous but the other person can have outside relationships.

OTHER TERMS IN USE

bonded: Without identifying the number of people involved, people who have forged emotional or sexual relationships sometimes use this term to show they are linked in some way. This could be done formally as well, with a commitment ceremony or handfasting including all those considering themselves to be bonded to one another in this way.

compersion: This is generally defined in poly circles as feeling happiness, warmth, or joy in another's pleasure, especially a lover's joy with their other lover(s).

friends with benefits: This is a casual sexual relationship between two people who do not see the relationship as being romantic or committed.

fluid bonded: Fluid bonding is the practice of sexual partners choosing to come in contact each other's bodily fluids. In multiple-partner situations, two people might be fluid bonded but insist lovers outside the fluid bond use protective measures (e.g., dental dams and condoms) to not share bodily fluids. A group of people might be fluid bonded to each other and have agreements not to make love to anyone outside the bond or to use protective measures if they do so. *See* screen.

ethical nonmonogamy: This term predates the term *polyamory*. It is the practice of having multiple sexual and/or romantic relationships with the consent and knowledge of all parties involved.

intimate network: This means the interconnections between all the people who are a person's sexual/emotional partners, and their partners. The depth of connection can be extended indefinitely.

life partner: This is a gender-neutral term often used by a couple who are in a sexual or romantic relationship that they regard as permanent. The couple can be married or unmarried. The term has also been used in a legal sense to refer to a domestic partner.

metamour: This is the person who is your lover's lover.

monogamy: Monogamy is an agreement between two people that they will have sex only with each other. The agreement may include prohibitions on building deep emotional or romantic bonds with outsiders as well.

monogamish: This term covers a range of attitudes and agreements within a committed relationship, sometimes described as "mostly monogamous." A couple makes agreements to be in a mostly exclusive relationship, but with clear agreements about when they can engage in nonmonogamous behavior and not be considered cheating.

nesting/nonnesting: A nesting partner is a live-in partner. This is a less emotionally charged term for some people than *primary* or *secondary*, denoting a higher level of emotional connection than a roommate.

new relationship energy (NRE): This is the feeling of being madly in love in a new romantic relationship. This feeling is quite common in a new relationship, but its appearance may be distressing to other partners of those involved in the new relationship. Good communication between all partners, new and old, is essential to prevent NRE from becoming toxic to established relationships.

polyamory: Polyamory is the practice of having multiple sexual and/or romantic relationships with the consent and knowledge of all parties involved.

semiresidential: This term is often used by people in a triadic or quad relationship who consider themselves primary to each other, with one or more persons in the relationship living in separate locations while still being a bonded part of the group.

solo polyamory: This is a person who follows the ethical rules of polyamory but makes it clear that they are not looking for a committed relationship with anyone. Solo polyamorous people value their independence and will sometimes say that they have a committed relationship only with themselves.

polycule: This term describes the connections or links between people involved intimately with each other, sometimes described as a network of people in polyamorous relationships. *See* intimate network.

polyfidelity: In this arrangement, all members in the group consider each other their primary partners and agree not to have any sexual or romantic relationships outside the group. The group is often residential and may or may not be open to including new members. *See* complex marriage.

POOSSLQ: This stands for Person of Opposite Sex Sharing Living Quarters. The rapidly changing sexual mores of the 1960s included large numbers of couples living together without the benefit of marriage. In the 1970s the US Census Bureau created this term to try to enumerate couples living together that did not define themselves as married.

screen: In the 1970s, the educational and residential organization Morehouse invented screening as a health tool for residents and participants in their community. Each person agrees to be medically tested for all known infectious and sexually transmitted diseases. After testing, the person agrees to not have any mucus membrane contact or share bodily fluids with anyone outside the screen. *See* fluid bonded.

significant other (SO): In polyamory, this is a gender-neutral term for a partner in an intimate relationship. The term does not impart any information like marital status, gender, or sex of the significant other.

other significant other (OSO): In psychology, an OSO could be any family member, friend, or other relationship that provides additional support that the significant other can't provide. In polyamory some people use this term to describe an additional sexual/emotional/romantic partner in a relationship, such as the third person joining a couple to make a triad.

Notes

CHAPTER 1

1. Morning Glory Zell-Ravenheart, "A Bouquet of Lovers," *Green Egg* 89 (1990).
2. Deborah M. Anapol, *Polyamory: The New Love without Limits: Secrets of Sustainable Intimate Relationships* (San Rafael, CA: Intinet Resource Center, 1997).
3. "John Humphrey Noyes, Complex Marriage, the Oneida Community," *Britannica*, http://www.Britannica.com/biography/John-Humphrey-Noyes#ref273760 (retrieved November 2021).
4. Morris Bishop, "The Great Onieda Love-in," *American Heritage* 20, no. 2 (February 1969).
5. "Mormon Fundamentalism Movement," *Wikipedia*, https://en.wikipedia.org/wiki/Mormon_fundamentalism (retrieved November 2021).
6. James White, ed., "Marriage among Indians," in *Handbook of Indians of Canada* (Ottawa, ON: Geographic Board of Canada, 1913), 275–76, http://faculty.marianopolis.edu/c.belanger/QuebecHistory/encyclopedia/IndianMarriage.htm (retrieved April 2022); "Marriage in Early Virginia Indian Society," *Encyclopedia Virginia*, https://encyclopediavirginia.org/entries/marriage-in-early-virginia-indian-society/ (retrieved November 2020).
7. Leanna Wolfe, *Women Who May Never Marry: The Reasons, Realities and Opportunities* (Atlanta, GA: Longstreet Press,1993).

CHAPTER 2

1. Deborah M. Anapol, *Polyamory: The New Love without Limits: Secrets of Sustainable Intimate Relationships* (San Rafael, CA: Intinet Resource Center, 1997).
2. Christopher Ryan and Cacilda Jetha, *Sex at Dawn: How We Mate, Why We Stray, and What It Means for Modern Relationships* (New York: HarperCollins, 2012), 134–37.

CHAPTER 3

1. Compersion is generally defined in poly circles as feeling happiness, warmth, or joy in another's pleasure, especially a lover's joy with their other lover(s).
2. "History of the DSM," American Psychiatric Association, http://www.psychia try.org/psychiatrists/practice/dsm/history-of-the-dsm (retrieved November 2020).
3. *Webster's Encyclopedic Unabridged Dictionary of the English Language* (New York: Dilithium Press, 1989).
4. Ibid.
5. "In Which States Is Cheating on Your Spouse Illegal?" *USA Today*, April 17, 2014.
6. Elisabeth Sheff, *The Polyamorists Next Door: Inside Multiple-Partner Relationships and Families* (Lanham, MD: Rowman & Littlefield, 2012), 38–44.
7. The invention of terms to describe what a person does or feels is a very powerful community-building tool. These terms have proven to be very beneficial to the many people in the polyamory community. Definitions can be found in the glossary.
8. Rachel Hope, *Family by Choice: Platonic Partnered Parenting* (N.p.: Word Birth Publishing, 2014).
9. Jessica Fern, *Polysecure: Attachment, Trauma and Consensual Nonmonogamy* (Portland, OR: Thorntree Press, 2021).
10. Kikue Fukami, *Shinsho 777 Polyamory Live a Multiple of Love* (N.p., Japan: Heibonsha Publisher, 2015); possibly only available in Japanese.

CHAPTER 4

1. Oxford English and Spanish Dictionary online, https://lexico.com/en/definition/synergy.
2. Quotes from Chayim and Pat Lafollette come from taped and in-person interviews with the authors.
3. Transcript reproduced as originally written by Terry Lee Brussel-Gibbons and Marcus Brussel Jenkins, with minor changes to enhance readability.

CHAPTER 5

1. Basic Sensuality, one of many courses in interpersonal relating and communicating Morehouse teaches, www.lafayettemorehouse.com (retrieved March 20, 2022).

2. Laurie Rivlin Heller, "Basic Sense: The More Philosophy of Victor Baranco and The Institute of Human Abilities," *Journal of the Communal Studies Association* 25 (2005).

3. Bob Schwartz and Leah Schwartz, *The One Hour Orgasm: How to Learn the Amazing "Venus Butterfly" Technique* (New York: St. Martin's Press, 2006).

4. Institute of OM, http://www.instituteofom.com; see also Institute of OM Foundation, https://iomfoundation.org.

5. Nellie Bowles, "Nicole Daedone's Mission of Orgasmic Meditation," *San Francisco Chronicle*, December 7, 2011, https://sfgate.com/living/article/Nicole-dadone-s-mission-of-orgasmic-meditation-2368554.php (retrieved April 2022); "Lafayette Morehouse," *Wikipedia*, https://en.wikipedia.org/wiki/lafayette_morehouse (retrieved March 20, 2022).

CHAPTER 6

1. More about Robert A. Heinlein can be found in the article titled "Heinlein Centennial" in the appendix.

2. William H. Patterson Jr. and Andrew Thorton, *The Martian Named Smith: Critical Perspectives on Robert A. Heinlein's* Stranger in a Strange Land (Citrus Heights, CA: Nitrosyncretic Press, 2001), back cover, 171–72.

3. Oberon Zell-Ravenheart and John C. Sulak, *The Wizard and the Witch* (Woodbury, MN: Llewellyn Publications, 2014), 273, 274.

4. Polyfidelity and compersion are terms invented by the Kerista Community and popularized by Ryam Nearing; see chapter 9.

CHAPTER 7

1. Excerpted from a Live the Dream newsletter article.

CHAPTER 8

1. Stan Dale and Val Beauchamp, *Fantasies Can Set You Free* (Millbrae, CA: Celestial Arts, 1980).

2. Human Awareness Institute (HAI), https://www1.hai.org.

3. Stan discusses opening his marriage in *Fantasies Can Set You Free*, 69–75.

4. Janet Dale, "Stan the Man," HAI Global Newsletter, June 8, 2012.
5. "Stan Dale Quotes," AZ Quotes, https://www.azquotes.com/author/45602-Stan
_Dale (accessed January 11, 2019).

CHAPTER 9

1. Alan M., "A History of Loving More," Loving More website, 2022 https://www
.lovingmorenonprofit.org/aboutus/history/ (retrieved March 25, 2022).
2. Ibid.
3. Deborah M. Anapol, *Love without Limits: The Quest for Sustainable Intimate
Relationships* (San Rafael, CA: Intinet Resource Center, 1992).
4. Deborah M. Anapol, *Polyamory: The New Love without Limits: Secrets of Sustainable Intimate Relationships* (San Rafael, CA: Intinet Resource Center, 1997).
5. Alan M., "History of Loving More."
6. Sasha Lessin and Janet Kira Lessin, *How to Really Love a Woman in Four Tantric
Trysts* (Bloomington, IN: AuthorHouse, 2011).

CHAPTER 10

1. Sex Positive Los Angeles, https://www.sexpositivelosangeles.org/about.
2. Sex Positive World, https://www.sexpositiveworld.org/.
3. Gabriella Cordova, YouTube https://www.youtube.com/channel/UC2utD_jD
luA3KzcJGY9SpEQ.

CHAPTER 11

1. Elisabeth A. Sheff, "How Many Polyamorists Are There in the U.S.?" *Psychology Today*, May 9, 2014, https://www.psychologytoday.com/us/blog/the-polyamorists
-next-door/201405/how-many-polyamorists-are-there-in-the-us (retrieved April 2022).
2. Rhonda N. Balzarini et al., "Demographic Comparison of American Individuals
in Polyamorous and Monogamous Relationships." *Journal of Sex Research* 56, no. 6
(June 18, 2018), https://www.tandfonline.com/doi/full/10.1080/00224499.2018.147
4333 (retrieved April 2022).
3. "Ethical Non-Monogamy: The Rise of Multi Partner Relationships," BBC
Worklife, https://www.bbc.com/worklife/article/20210326-ethical-non-monogamy
-the-rise-of-multi-partner-relationships (retrieved November 2020).
4. Ellen Barry, "A Massachusetts City Decides to Recognize Polyamorous Relationships," *New York Times*, July 1, 2020, https://www.nytimes.com/2020/07/01/us
/somerville-polyamorous-domestic-partnership.html (retrieved April 2022).

Bibliography

Anapol, Deborah M. *Love without Limits: The Quest for Sustainable Intimate Relationships*. San Rafael, CA: Intinet Resource Center, 1992.

———. *Polyamory: The New Love without Limits: Secrets of Sustainable Intimate Relationships*. San Rafael, CA: Intinet Resource Center, 1997.

Balzarini, Rhonda N., Christoffer Dharma, Taylor Kohut, Bjarne M. Holmes, Lorne Campbell, Justin J. Lehmiller, and Jennifer J. Harman. "Demographic Comparison of American Individuals in Polyamorous and Monogamous Relationships." *Journal of Sex Research* 56, no. 6 (June 18, 2018). https://www.tandfonline.com/doi/full/10.1080/00224499.2018.1474333. Retrieved April 2022.

Barry, Ellen. "A Massachusetts City Decides to Recognize Polyamorous Relationships." *New York Times*, July 1, 2020. https://www.nytimes.com/2020/07/01/us/somerville-polyamorous-domestic-partnership.html. Retrieved April 2022.

Bishop, Morris. "The Great Onieda Love-in." *American Heritage* 20, no. 2 (February 1969).

Bowles, Nellie. "Nicole Daedone's Mission of Orgasmic Meditation." *San Francisco Chronicle*, December 7, 2011. https:sfgate.com/living/article/Nicole-dadone-s-mission-of-orgasmic-meditation-2368554.php. Retrieved April 2022.

Constantine, Larry L., and Joan M. Constantine. *Group Marriage: A Study of Contemporary Multilateral Marriage*. New York: Collier Books, 1973.

Dale, Janet. "Stan the Man." HAI Global Newsletter, June 8, 2012.

Dale, Stan. *My Child, My Self: How to Raise the Child You Always Wanted to Be*. Millbrae, CA: Human Awareness Publications, 1992.

Dale, Stan, and Val Beaucham. *Fantasies Can Set You Free*. Millbrae, CA: Celestial Arts, 1980.

"Ethical Non-Monogamy: The Rise of Multi Partner Relationships." BBC Worklife. https://www.bbc.com/worklife/article/20210326-ethical-non-monogamy-the-rise -of-multi-partner-relationships. Retrieved November 2020.

Heller, Laurie Rivlin. "Basic Sense: The More Philosophy of Victor Baranco and the Insitiute of Human Abilities." *Journal of the Communal Studies Association* 25 (2005).

Heraclitus. Translated from a fragment of his one known work. All discovered fragments of his work are without titles. It is not known if this work ever had a title. https://en.wikipedia.org/wiki/heraclitus and https://www.azquotes.com/author /19778-heraclitus.

"History of the DSM." American Psychiatric Association. http://www.psychiatry.org /psychiatrists/practice/dsm/history-of-the-dsm. Retrieved November 2020.

"In Which States Is Cheating on Your Spouse Illegal?" *USA Today*, April 17, 2014.

"John Humphrey Noyes, Complex Marriage, the Oneida Community." *Britannica.* http://www.Britannica.com/biography/John-Humphrey-Noyes#ref273760. Retrieved November 2021.

"Marriage in Early Virginia Indian Society." *Encyclopedia Virginia.* https://encyclopedia virginia.org/entries/marriage-in-early-virginia-indian-society/. Retrieved November 2020.

"Mormon Fundamentalism Movement." *Wikipedia.* https://en.wikipedia.org/wiki /Mormon_fundamentalism. Retrieved November 2021.

Patterson, William H., Jr., and Andrew Thorton. *The Martian Named Smith: Critical Perspectives on Robert A. Heinlein's Stranger in a Strange Land.* Sacramento, CA: Nitrosyncretic Press, 2001.

Ryan, Christopher, and Cacilda Jetha. *Sex at Dawn: How We Mate, Why We Stray, and What It Means for Modern Relationships.* New York: HarperCollins, 2012.

Schwartz, Bob, and Leah Schwartz. *The One Hour Orgasm: How to Learn the Amazing "Venus Butterfly" Technique.* New York: St. Martin's Press, 2006.

Sheff, Elisabeth A. "How Many Polyamorists Are There in the U.S.?" *Psychology Today,* May 9, 2014. https://www.psychologytoday.com/us/blog/the-polyamorists-next -door/201405/how-many-polyamorists-are-there-in-the-u.s. Retrieved April 2022.

Sheff, Elisabeth. *The Polyamorists Next Door: Inside Multiple-Partner Relationships and Families.* Lanham, MD: Rowman & Littlefield, 2012.

Webster's Encyclopedic Unabridged Dictionary of the English Language. New York: Dilithium Press, 1989.

White, James, ed. "Marriage among Indians." In *Handbook of Indians of Canada*, 275– 76. Ottawa, ON: Geographic Board of Canada, 1913. http://faculty.marianopolis .edu/c.belanger/QuebecHistory/encyclopedia/IndianMarriage.htm. Retrieved April 2022.

Wolfe, Leanna. *Women Who May Never Marry: The Reasons, Realities and Opportunities.* Atlanta, GA: Longstreet Press, 1993.

Zane, Zachary. "Who Really Practices Polyamory?" *Rolling Stones*, November 12, 2018.

Zell-Ravenheart, Morning Glory. "A Bouquet of Lovers." *Green Egg* 89 (1990).

Zell-Ravenheart, Oberon, ed. *Green Egg Omelette: An Anthology of Art and Articles from the Legendary Pagan Journal.* Franklin Lakes, NJ: New Page Books, 2009.

Zell-Ravenheart, Oberon, and John C. Sulak. *The Wizard and the Witch.* Woodbury, MN: Llewellyn Publications, 2014.

SUGGESTED READING

Anapol, Deborah. *Polyamory in the 21st Century: Love and Intimacy with Multiple Partners*. Lanham, MD: Rowman & Littlefield, 2010.

Brussel-Rogers, Terry L. *Matchmaker's Corner: Choosing, Finding, and Attracting Your Life Mate*. Los Angeles, CA: Success Center, 1990.

Dale, Stan. *My Child, My Self: How to Raise the Child You Always Wanted to Be*. San Mateo, CA: Human Awareness Publications, 1992.

Fern, Jessica. *Polysecure: Attachment, Trauma and Consensual Nonmonogamy*. Portland, OR: Thorntree Press, 2021.

Fukami, Kikue. *Shinsho 777 Polyamory Live a Multiple of Love*. N.p., Japan: Heibonsha Publisher, 2015. Possibly only available in Japanese.

Hardy, Janet W., and Dossie Easton. *The Ethical Slut: A Practical Guide to Polyamory, Open Relationships, and Other Freedoms in Sex and Love*, 3rd edition. Berkeley, CA: Ten Speed Press, 2017.

Heinlein, Robert A. *Stranger in a Stranger Land*. New York: Ace Books, 1961.

Hope, Rachel. *Family by Choice: Platonic Partnered Parenting*. Los Angeles, CA: Family by Choice, 2014.

Jenkins, Ian. *Three Dads and a Baby: Adventures in Modern Parenting*. Hoboken, NJ: Cleis Press, 2021.

Labriola, Kathy. *The Jealousy Workbook: Exercises and Insights for Managing Open Relationships*. Emeryville, CA: Greenery Press, 2013.

Lessin, Sasha, and Janet Kira Lessin. *How to Really Love a Woman in Four Tantric Trysts*. Bloomington, IN: AuthorHouse, 2011.

Nearing, Ryam. *Loving More: The Polyfidelity Primer*. Eugene, OR: PEP Publishing, 1992.

Patterson, William H. *Robert A. Heinlein: In Dialogue with His Century, Vol. 1— Learning Curve (1907–1948)*. New York: Tor Books, 2010.

Rimmer, Robert. *The Harrad Experiment*. Los Angeles, CA: Sherbourne Press, 1966.

Sheff, Elisabeth. *Stories from the Polycule: Real Life in Polyamorous Families*. Portland, OR: Thorntree Press, 2015.

Veaux, Franklin, and Eve Rickert. *More Than Two: A Practical Guide to Ethical Polyamory*. Portland, OR: Thorntree Press, 2014.

Winston, Dedeker. *The Smart Girl's Guide to Polyamory: Everything You Need to Know about Open Relationships, Non-Monogamy and Alternative Love*. New York: Skyhorse Publishing, 2017.

ORGANIZATIONS OF INTEREST

Church of All Worlds, http://www.caw.org
Family Tree (Boston area), https://polyfamilytree.org
Human Awareness Institute (HAI), https://www1.hai.org

Institute of Human Abilities (Morehouse), https://oaklandmorehouse.com
Institute of OM, http://www.instituteofom.com
Live the Dream, https://www.livethedream.org
Loving More, http://www.lovingmorenonprofit.org
Sex Positive Los Angeles, http://www.meetup.com/Sex-Positive-LA/
Sex Positive World, https://www.sexpositiveworld.org/

Index

Abundant Love Institute, 68
acceptance, 43
accidental polyamory, 23–25
activism
    attitudes and beliefs regarding sex, 14
    child rearing and, 75–76
    gay rights organizations, 75–76, 94–95
    legal positions regarding sex and marriage and, 15–16
    Sex Positive World (SPW) and, 94–95
    Summer of Love (1967), 3–4
adultery, 17
Allot House, 72–73
"Alternative Dating Etiquette" (Brussel-Rogers), 109–14
American Psychiatric Association (APA), 14–15
Anapol, Dr. Deborah, 10, 24, 61, 68, 87
    Loving More and, 85–92
    relationship configurations, 31
    terminology and, 1, 7
animal models, 10–11
anthropology, 10–11

antiwar movement of the 1960s and 1970s, 3–4, 43
anxious attachment, 22–23
associations. *See individual associations*
attachment and attachment theory, 22–23

Balzarini, Dr. Rhonda, 100
Baranco, Dr. Cynthia, 52
Baranco, Dr. Suzanne, 10, 49
Baranco, Dr. Victor, 10, 47–52, 53–54
Basic Sense course, 48, 49–50
    See also Morehouse
Beat culture of the 1950s, 4, 56
bigamy, 16
biological factors, 10–11, 22–23
bisexuality
    "Bouquet of Lovers" article (Zell-Ravenheart), 66
    Live the Dream organization and, 74–75
    Loving More and, 89, 90
bodily fluids, 52, 125
"The Body Sacred" conference, 87
bonded, 125

137

"How Does a Poly Person Find Time
   Enough for Love" (Brussel-Rogers),
   114–16
Human Awareness Institute (HAI)
   intimacy workshops and, 81–83
   keynote address at the 2006 Family
   Synergy Annual Convention, 43
   overview, 10, 79–83
Human Awareness Movement, 56
Human Potential Movement, 4, 56, 72
hypersexuality disorder, 14–15
hypnosis and hypnotherapy, 42, 89

illegality. *See* laws and legal factors
indigenous populations, 3
informed consent, 94, 96, 97–98
inheritance rights, 16–17
Institute for Advanced Study of Human
   Sexuality, 47
Institute of Human Abilities, 49
   See also Morehouse
Intentional Communities, 59
interpersonal communication. *See*
   communication
interracial marriage, 15–16, 94–95, 101
intimacy, 19–20, 79–83
intimate network, 126
IntiNet Resource Center, 86–87, 88
Iroquois Confederacy, 3

Japanese culture, 24–25
jealousy
   "Bouquet of Lovers" article (Zell-
      Ravenheart), 65–66
   Family Synergy workshops regarding,
      33, 34
   keynote address at the 2006 Family
      Synergy Annual Convention, 43
   Live the Dream organization and,
      76
   reasons given for adopting a poly
      lifestyle and, 22–23
Jenkins, Ian, 101

Kerista Community
   Loving More and, 89
   overview, 85–86
   PEPCon and, 61–62, 87
Kink/BDSM community, 76
Kinsey, Alfred, 47
Kirkridge Retreat Center convention, 88

Lafollette, Ann, 28–35, 105–9
Lafollette, Pat, 28–35, 39, 70, 106–9
laws and legal factors
   adultery laws, 17
   bigamy laws, 16–17
   homosexuality and same-sex
      marriage, 16
   marriage and, 101
   overview, 15–18
   parental rights and, 101
   Sex Positive World (SPW) and,
      94–95
Lessin, Janet, 92
Lessin, Sasha, 92
life partner, 126
line marriage, 58, 62, 121
Live the Dream organization
   Church of All Worlds and, 58–59
   Family Synergy and, 42, 44–45
   Loving More and, 89
   meetings and events, 71–73, 76–77
   newsletter from, 58–59, 69, 73–74,
      90–91, 103–5, 109–21
   origins of, 69–71, 105
   overview, 10, 71–77
   Sex Positive World (SPW) and, 97
love, 20, 22–23, 43
Love without Limits (Anapol), 86
Love Without Limits workshops, 10
Loving Choices seminars, 91
Loving More
   conventions, 42, 85, 88–91, 92
   keynote address at the 2006 Family
      Synergy Annual Convention, 42
   origins of, 85–89

About the Authors

Glen W. Olson is an author and historian of the polyamory movement and gives presentations on the history of polyamory to interested groups. He is a retired fire captain, paramedic, and technical writer. He is a contributing author to the Los Angeles Fire Department's original CERT Disaster Preparedness Student Manual, distributed nationwide by FEMA. He has written several student manuals for internal fire department use and is a published fiction writer. His introduction to organized polyamory began in the 1970s when he was invited to attend a workshop on open relationships at Elysium Fields in Topanga Canyon, California. The workshop was hosted by the organization Family Synergy. He subsequently joined Family Synergy, attending many workshops and conventions. Over the next several decades he attended events put on by almost every organization on the West Coast and several in the Midwest and eastern United States. Over the years he has made presentations to colleges and interested groups like science fiction conventions on the subject of open relationships and polyamory.

Terry Lee Brussel-Rogers is a certified clinical hypnotherapist and life/business coach, director of Success Center Inc. since 1969. She has a BA in psychology and eight additional years of training in hypnotherapy. Terry is a fourth-generation matchmaker (poly and monogamous) who ran Marriage Minded Introductions for forty years. She has done poly relationship coaching including sensitivity training and jealousy workshops since 1971. She was on the board of Family Synergy off and on from 1982 through 2011, frequently handling education and outreach as well as event planning. She won the Life Styles Award for Contributing to the Knowledge of Human Sexuality in 1988 for her alternative lifestyle workshops, poly counseling, and such hypnotic recordings as "Male Multiple Orgasm," "Intimacy without Jealousy," and "Sexual Enhancement for Couples." In 1987, Terry founded Live the Dream for those who, originally inspired by the writings of science fiction such as Robert Heinlein's *Stranger in a Strange Land*, are ready to live such alternative lifestyles as multiply committed relationships, group marriage, and group living. Live the Dream is still meeting regularly at this writing. It is also the Los Angeles Nest of Church of All Worlds, the first legally recognized Neo-Pagan religion in the United States.

CPSIA information can be obtained
at www.ICGtesting.com
Printed in the USA
BVHW042029040822
643762BV00001B/1